Is the Open Society Sust
Case of Emergency?

IS THE OPEN SOCIETY SUSTAINABLE IN CASE OF EMERGENCY?

A Convoco Edition

CORINNE MICHAELA FLICK (ED.)

Convoco! Editions

Copyright © for the texts by the authors
and Convoco Foundation 2024

The rights of the named authors to be identified as the authors of this
work have been asserted in accordance with the Copyright,
Designs and Patents Act, 1988.

The publisher has used its best endeavors to ensure that the URLs for
external websites referred to in this book are correct and active at the
time of going to press. However, the publisher has no responsibility for
the websites and can make no guarantee that a site will remain live or
that the content is or will remain appropriate.

Convoco Foundation
Brienner Strasse 28
D – 80333 Munich
www.convoco.co.uk

British Library Cataloguing-in-Publication data: a catalogue
record for this book is available from the British Library.

Edited by Dr. Corinne Michaela Flick
Translated from German by Philippa Hurd
Layout and typesetting by Jill Sawyer Phypers
Printed and bound in Great Britain by Clays Ltd, Elcograf S.p.A.

ISBN: 978-1-9163673-8-8

Previously published Convoco titles:

Equality in an Unequal World (2023)

How much Freedom must we Forgo to be Free? (2022)

New Global Alliances: Institutions, Alignments and Legitimacy in the Contemporary World (2021)

The Standing of Europe in the New Imperial World Order (2020)

The Multiple Futures of Capitalism (2019)

The Common Good in the 21st Century (2018)

Authority in Transformation (2017)

Power and its Paradoxes (2016)

To Do or Not To Do—Inaction as a Form of Action (2015)

Dealing with Downturns: Strategies in Uncertain Times (2014)

Collective Law-Breaking—A Threat to Liberty (2013)

Who Owns the World's Knowledge? (2012)

*Yet where danger lies,
grows that which saves.*

Friedrich Hölderlin (1770–1843)

CONTENTS

Introduction   1
Theses   9

1. Europe in Crisis Mode: 15
   Lessons from the Most Recent Past
   Moritz Schularick

2. The Case of Emergency as a Crisis of   31
   Governance and Legitimation:
   A Historical Perspective
   Jörn Leonhard

3. Is the Western Institutional Consensus   49
   Sustainable?
   Marietta Auer

4. Perhaps It Is Time to Stop Thinking in   73
   Terms of the West
   Tim Crane

5. Democracy at Risk, the Law at Risk — 81
Stefan Korioth

6. The Neurobiology of Trust — 97
Martin Korte

7. What Accounts for a Democratic State's Ability to Defend its Core Values? — 113
Birke Häcker

8. Democracy in Danger? — 135
Peter M. Huber

9. Have Capitalist Economic Institutions Functioned During the Crisis? — 163
Monika Schnitzer

10. Climate Change Changes Everything — 179
Wolfgang Schön

11. Economic Development and Sustainability — 191
Clemens Fuest

12. Transform Yourself — 205
Timo Meynhardt

13. Relations, Networks, and Entanglements: 227
    The Anthropocene as a Challenge
    to Modern Democratic Governance
    in Europe
    Claudia Wiesner

14. The International Trading System in 245
    Turmoil: From a Positive-Sum Game to
    a Zero-Sum Game—and Back Again?
    Gabriel Felbermayr

15. Crisis as the Antidote to Boredom 281
    Adrian Ghenie & Hans Ulrich Obrist
    in Conversation

    Contributors 301

INTRODUCTION

Dear Friends of Convoco,

It is now obvious that we are living in a time of unusually wide-ranging upheaval. Many of the assumptions we have relied upon have become problematic or are no longer valid. These changes beg the question as to the state of the systems that shape the world.

We deliberately used the word "emergency"[1] in the title of this volume, rather than "crisis," because we want to make it clear that the crisis stage may be behind us and that we have already entered the emergency phase. What is certain is that the situation today is more serious and dangerous than it was five years ago. Since 2008, various crises have constantly followed and overlapped one another. The historian Adam Tooze has popularized the term "polycrisis" to describe this grey area between crisis and emergency.[2] At the same time, we are experiencing a difficult situation that has not existed in this form in the last 50 years. In the West, we are faced with a high level of polarization in society, accompanied by the sense that Western democracies are no longer stable. Above all, there are significant differences between individual democracies. The West is no longer unified. There are legitimate doubts as to whether "the West" will even continue to exist in the future as the entity we currently know.[3] The focus is on the major issue of the climate crisis, the loss of biodiversity, a growing rivalry between the US and China, and two wars that no one expected (although hindsight suggests they should have been foreseeable). Even if all of these challenges are recognized, the extent and ramifications of our current plight are not manageable or identifiable for individuals. Compounding today's problems is the fact that we are experiencing dramatic technological innovations. The age of artificial intelligence has dawned and it is putting institutions and systems to the test. In this situation it is important to be aware that the more technological innovations are introduced, the greater the uncertainty about the future will be.

And that brings us to the actual question of this volume: "Are the systems sustainable?" By "systems" we mean the social, legal, governmental, and diplomatic structures of societies and states. Our focus is not just on Western systems. Nevertheless, these are inevitably in the foreground, because from 1800 until the start of this millennium the West has steadily grown in importance and its institutions have dominated the world's social fabric. After World War II, the US's hegemony was absolute. During this phase, a number of institutions emerged that created a post-war "rules-based international order" and, although subject to many challenges, these continue to structure the world today. These institutions include the United Nations (UN), the World Bank, the International Monetary Fund (IMF), the North Atlantic Treaty Organization (NATO), the General Agreement on Tariffs and Trade (GATT), the Organization for Economic Co-operation and Development (OECD), and the Group of the Seven (G7). These institutions underpin, with varying degrees of effectiveness, the principles of the market economy, freedom, democracy, respect for national sovereignty, and the multilateral order. The idea behind this move to create a rules-based world was to ensure free trade, maintain international order, and to promote ideas of justice – even in institutions (such as the UN) where not all nation states were committed to such ideals. Symbolically, the West has been seen to stand for a system of values and ideas such as freedom and human rights: a universal message, even if it is one that also needs to be judged critically in light of its own history of colonialism and past oppressions.

In terms of the share of global gross national product, the Western system's dominance peaked economically in 1999.

What is being tested today is the existence and legitimacy of the central institutions of the liberal, enlightened, institutional consensus that has its origins the 18th century and which has been exemplified by the international rules-based order as it has been promoted by the West since 1945.

- Challenges to this rules-based system come from a multitude of sources. The rule of law is threatened by political overreach and an increase in political extremism from both right and left.

- With a dismantling of the rule of law comes the weakening of the fundamental rights enshrined in those nations' constitutions. The media and the public sphere as a whole are also coming under increasing pressure from this political polarization, from fake news, and the emergence of "parallel worlds" and online "bubbles."

- Democracy is faced with a great deal of dissatisfaction and increasing populism internally, and simultaneously has to assert itself against autocratic systems externally. This puts its form of government at risk.

- The social market economy is being called into question by growing inequalities, new ideologies, and by poor economic policy decisions that have failed to deliver improvements in living standards for large sections of the Western populations. This poses a threat to private autonomy, which in turn is the basis of the capitalist economic system.

- Rational policy choices in politics in general are increasingly being neglected as a result of pressures from many sources, including populism, disinformation, and religious extremism. Science is also at risk from falsification. Artificial intelligence is one of the biggest challenges in this respect.

- International cooperation is coming under increasing pressure due to the systemic conflict between the US and China, geopolitical conflicts of interest, and scarcity of resources. Above all, the natural world is under acute threat. It is important to recognize that human life on earth itself is in danger.

At this point various questions arise:

- Are the systems that form the basis of our world resilient? Are they sustainable and at the same time flexible enough to change so that they can continue to fulfill their functions into the future? Nothing is more difficult than getting institutions to change. But that doesn't mean it's impossible.

- Are the institutions, many of which date back to the 18th century or at least to the bipolar world of 1945–1989, obsolete? Do they still relate to the global world order as it is in 2024?

- In the West, are we as a society capable of adapting and can we adapt to the changed situation and challenges quickly enough? Do we have the necessary flexibility and openness to change the way we think and live? The subject of sacrifice arises, both on a personal and collective level.[4] But is it really about sacrificing today or is it more about taking a long-term perspective and recalibrating our goals and scale of values? Throughout history, the concept of sacrifice has not always had negative connotations.[5]

The consensus that emerges from these essays is that our challenge is to preserve what's good about the existing systems while adapting them at the same time. The history of empires shows—leaving open the question of whether the West represents an empire in the classic sense—that change is essential for, but not always sufficient for, survival. At least some of the lessons of the past are now self-evident.

The various partners and elements of a system are constantly changing their relationship to one another. And so the system as a whole changes. Shifts in economic power entail shifts in political power. Whether the Western-style systems are sustainable depends on us as a society being prepared and brave enough to embrace change—and smart enough to choose the right kind of change. Nevertheless, societal change alone is no guarantee for success. Concrete ideas and solutions are needed. In this volume, many of the contributors offer suggestions on what measures can improve the situation. For example, Moritz Schularick and Monika Schnitzer argue for significant investments in state capacity in order to increase crisis resilience; Martin Korte encourages us to rethink political communication according to today's insights from neurobiology; and Peter M. Huber suggests reforms to revitalize our democratic institutions. The essays that follow do not pretend to offer any simple solutions. But for those of us who seek to preserve the rules-based international order and the liberal democratic values that inspired it, these essays offer at least the beginnings of an answer to the question of how that elusive goal might be achieved.

Corinne Michaela Flick, January 2024

Notes

1. See Bazon Brock, "Selbstfesselungskünstler zwischen Gottsucherbanden und Unterhaltungsidioten: Für eine Kultur diesseits des Ernstfalls und jenseits von Macht, Geld und Unsterblichkeit" in Bazon Brock, Die Re-Dekade (Munich: Klinkhardt und Biermann, 1989), pp. 127-252, https://bazonbrock.de/werke/detail/?id=32&sectid=54 (accessed March 22, 2024).

2. Adam Tooze, "Welcome to the World of the Polycrisis," *Financial Times*, October 28, 2022, https://www.ft.com/content/498398e7-11b1-494b-9cd3-6d669dc3de33 (accessed May 13, 2024).

3. Cf. Tim Crane, pp. 76–78, in the present volume.

4. Convoco discussed the topic inaction as a form of action back in 2014. Inaction always involves a sacrifice. See: Corinne Michaela Flick (ed.), *To Do or Not To Do – Inaction as a Form of Action* (Göttingen: Wallstein, 2015).

5. Cf. Otfried Höffe, *Die hohe Kunst des Verzichts* (Munich: C.H. Beck, 2023), pp. 24–25.

THESES

MORITZ SCHULARICK

Crises are the new normal of our era. The pandemic alongside the wars in Ukraine and in the Middle East are symptoms of a new world order that increasingly demands resilience. Germany must build up and expand its competence in dealing with economic crises in order to remain competitive on the international stage and avoid unnecessary costs.

MARIETTA AUER

Individual and political autonomy, the crucial pillars of the liberal model of society, are only possible within a general climate of societal liberalism that consistently defends itself against new forms of totalitarianism.

BIRKE HÄCKER

The ability of a democratic state to defend its core values rests on a combination of factors: constitutional provisions protecting it against being undermined "from within," and societal factors operating "from outwith" which cannot ultimately be guaranteed by the state of its constitution. Both elements—"internal" as well as "external" factors—help stabilize democracy and the rule of law, even in the case of emergency.

PETER M. HUBER

Germany currently does neither suffer from a state crisis nor is the constitutional order in danger. There is still a broad social consensus in favor of a liberal democracy contained by the rule of law. However, the success of the constitutional state since 1949 is no reason to rest on our laurels, because there exist phenomena that cast shadows over the reassuring picture.

STEFAN KORIOTH

Democracy is the transformational form of government. Crucial to this form is a specific, albeit fragile, combination of stability and openness, of deliberation and decision-making, of democratic forms and law in the constitutional state.

MARTIN KORTE

Trust is essential in every social interaction. Trust is strengthened when we believe in the authenticity of those in charge, and when people in stressful situations still think that they have scope for action. Fear, by contrast, limits the brain's processing capacity.

MONIKA SCHNITZER

Whether the state can fulfil its task of coordinating between actors in crisis situations depends largely on state capacity. Improving public administration and governance must therefore be the top priority.

WOLFGANG SCHÖN

A healthy climate isn't everything, but everything is nothing without a healthy climate. Only if we succeed in stabilizing the global climate system will we have a chance of maintaining the resilience of our other systems.

CLEMENS FUEST

Focusing technical and social progress on environmental protection, combined with investments in the regeneration and preservation of natural capital, is the more promising route to sustainability than a reduction in economic output.

HANS ULRICH OBRIST

Artworks and exhibitions are traveling around the world and have an environmental impact, which creates the question whether it would be more sustainable and therefore necessary to find more fixed places for art. I see many artists right now who say, metaphorically speaking, that they would rather make a garden than an exhibition. It's about long durational projects.

TIMO MEYNHARDT

Individual well-being and the common good are interdependent, in a sense existentially intertwined, and fundamentally inseparable. We live within a system and live by drawing upon a system. This relationship between the self and the world is where our scope for creativity lies.

CLAUDIA WIESNER

The goal for governing democratically in the Anthropocene would be to embrace complexity and relationality, to search for networked solutions, to think in entanglements, and to give up on hunting linear causalities.

TIM CRANE

We shouldn't think that the threat to the global or liberal world order is a threat to the values that it's trying to promote.

GABRIEL FELBERMAYR

The international trading system should not be seen structurally as in a de-globalization phase, but rather in a transformation phase. This includes the creation of blocs. But there is also something positive behind this creation of blocs, namely the search for models that work.

CORINNE M. FLICK

Our challenge is to preserve what's good about the existing systems and adapting them at the same time. Change is essential for survival. We have to acknowledge that the world as it appeared in the 19th and 20th centuries is disappearing. Whether the Western-style systems are sustainable depends on all of us.

JÖRN LEONHARD

A case of emergency is always also an opportunity that recalls the fundamentally open meaning of "crisis"—not as a negative characterization of an event, but as a decision-making phase whose outcome is open.

ADRIAN GHENIE

We are only doing art because we are in crisis. There is no art without crisis.

CHAPTER 1

EUROPE IN CRISIS MODE: LESSONS FROM THE MOST RECENT PAST

MORITZ SCHULARICK

Polities and economies get into crisis states again and again.[1] Economic crises and the political reactions to them are a central topic in my research agenda. How such crises can be prevented and whether they can be predicted – these questions were the core of an essay I wrote in 2012. "His research developed a more fundamental understanding of crisis dynamics that can help predict and mitigate future crises," said the laudation for the Leibniz Prize that the German Research Foundation awarded to me for this essay in 2021. I wish I could even begin to share this optimistic assessment.

We still know very little about the dynamics and causes of economic crises. Crisis issues have stuck with me, especially the question of the political responses to crises. What do we know about successful crisis management from a scientific perspective? What works and why? How do we manage to make the right decisions in crisis-dictated real time and get the knowledge to the decision-makers quickly?

My research was mainly about the crises in the financial sector, which I know best: financial crises, such as we had in March 2023, when Silicon Valley Bank collapsed in the US and a few days later Credit Suisse went belly up in Switzerland. In this crisis, central banks used the freedom offered by a flexible monetary currency and provided enough liquidity to financial institutions so that all investors got their money back. Among them were many tech companies and a few billionaires like Peter Thiel, who unsuspectingly had many millions in their accounts.

The storm passed, the stock market prices wobbled briefly, but things quickly picked up again. Was that the right reaction of the central banks, was the crisis management successful? From a macroeconomic perspective, yes. The crisis was over, the collapse averted.

But criticism was not long in coming. Should taxpayers' money really be used to protect the assets of large investors? Where were the incentives for better behavior in the future, where was liability and responsibility? Was the crisis management successful in the short term, but dangerous in the medium term as misbehavior was programmed into the future? Ultimately do central banks have to run faster and faster in the end just to stand still? What is optimal crisis management?

With the war in Ukraine, an emergency occurred in Europe in 2022. There were three major decisions that Germany had to make, issues of paramount importance for peace and freedom in Europe:

1. Would Russia attack Ukraine?

2. Would Ukraine be able to defend itself successfully?

3. Would Germany be able to break away from its gas dependence on Russia at moderate economic costs and thus be able to act with a free hand in foreign policy?

The answer of Berlin's politicians to these questions was: no, no, no. The correct answers would have been: yes, yes, yes.

In other words, we were wrong in what were probably the most important questions Germany has had to answer in the last 30 years since reunification. It took time and gambled away a lot of trust with allies and also a lot of money to then correct these misjudgments bit by bit. The result was a policy that was too hesitant for a very long time, because it started from false premises, fearing the end of gas supplies and the risk of blackmail.

Berlin was visibly impressed by Putin's threats and by the warnings of national interest groups. In the end, it was Putin, not a strategically acting German foreign policy, who brought about the end of gas imports. Rather, German foreign policy hid behind the interests of some companies and industries.

The third question, whether Germany could break away from its gas dependence on Russia, was a debate that directly affected the economy. It was the subject of a heated debate between mainly academic economists and the representatives of interest groups and their think tanks.

In the public discussion there was talk of mass poverty and popular uprisings. The CEO of Germany's largest chemical company asked whether we want to destroy our entire national economy with our eyes open. The Institute of the German Economy, financed by business associations, considered 2.5 to 3 million additional unemployed people quite conceivable. The leadership of the Federation of German Industries (BDI) saw the country's substance threatened. But the trade unions too got involved and produced alarmist studies.

In reality, the adjustment worked without major disruptions. Germany consumed about 20 percent less gas last year than in the previous year. Additional supplies from other countries, not least liquefied natural gas (LNG) from the US, have provided the rest.

At the heart of the successful adjustment was the price mechanism, the backbone of the market economy, its real strength. Many economists have underestimated this. The price signal travels through the system and leads to adjustments where they are easiest to achieve. The market produces knowledge that no government has. We have distrusted this mechanism and, as a consequence, have made crisis policy under false pretenses. This insight that we have no better mechanism than the market to allocate scarce goods is something we need to remember especially for climate transformation.

To this day, the myth persists that the halt to gas deliveries to Germany and Europe came at a fortunate time: for example, with warm temperatures in winter. The opposite is true. If one could have chosen a year to cause maximum damage by ending gas supplies, it was 2022.

French nuclear power plants went off the grid and the drought in Europe caused a dramatic drop in electricity production by hydroelectric power plants. Moreover, last year was not much warmer than expected. And the warm days were mainly in October and November when the storage tanks were already full. The average temperature in winter 2022/23 was 2.9 degrees Celsius, compared to more than 3 degrees Celsius last year, in line overall with the trend of a warming continent.

Could even an earlier embargo have been tolerated? We know that too today: the answer is yes. The calculation is simple—and in the end it was not even close. At the end of the heating period, there were still 160 TwH of gas in the storage tanks. Around 100 TwH still came from Russia between March and July 2022. Even without Russian gas, the storage facilities would still have been a quarter full at the end of the winter.

The bottom line is that Germany escaped with a black eye, but not because it was particularly competent in crisis management. The LNG terminals, which were built in record time, are certainly an exception, and things also worked well at the operational level. But when it comes to the central strategic questions of 2022,

German politics has long been based on false premises. Actions were guided by erroneous assumptions that tied Germany's hands in essential security questions.

I think there is a more fundamental problem here. Germany is not particularly competent in crisis thinking and crisis management—neither currently nor historically—with serious consequences. The development of crisis competence is central to mastering the challenges of the coming decades. Currently the term resilience is much discussed, i.e. the ability to deal with shocks. Resilience prominently includes political crisis competence.

We wouldn't have to worry about lacking crisis competence if crises were only rare occurrences. However, the frequency of crises has increased massively over the last two decades and we will not be able to return to normality any time soon. And then it will cost Germany dearly for its poor economic crisis management.

Of course, the questions that arise in crises are not always the same. History doesn't repeat itself, it rhymes, to paraphrase Mark Twain. But the idea that, when the terrible Russian war of aggression is over, we will return to some kind of normality, is naive. And recent events in the Middle East and society's reactions to them confirm my assumption. The crises are lining up.

The historian Adam Tooze uses the word "polycrisis" to describe the overlapping crises in different areas of our lives—environment, security, politics, economics, technology, migration—the list of challenges is long.

Former US Treasury Secretary Lawrence Summers recently remarked on climate transformation: "This is the most complex, diverse, and multilayered challenge that I can remember in the 40 years I've been paying attention to such things."[2] Or as the recently deceased French philosopher Bruno Latour put it during the COVID-19 pandemic: this is all just a dress rehearsal for the climate crisis we are facing.[3]

Irreversible interventions in the planet's ecological budget will not only lead to further natural disasters, pandemics, and droughts, but also to waves of migration and political conflicts between and within societies. In the age of polycrisis, my thesis is that crisis competence is extremely important and even a competitive advantage.

If you really want to get scared, look at the state of the Western democracies, that is, our political governance mechanisms, at the beginning of this polycrisis. In the US, Great Britain, France, Israel, and Italy, the party system has massively slipped and populists are on the rise, increasingly in Germany as well. The proportion of countries governed by populists is at an all-time high of around 25 percent.

But where are the deficits in Germany right now? During the pandemic, the Scientific Advisory Board of the Federal Ministry of Economics diagnosed "structures, processes and ways of thinking that seem archaic in parts" and did not hesitate to speak of "organizational failure" in an official report.[4] Sixty percent of Germans believed that the state was unable to fulfill its tasks. At that time, as I summarized it in the title of a book, the state was disenchanted, and this had severe consequences: dissatisfaction, declining legitimacy, protest, and political apathy.

It is also illuminating to look at the last major economic crisis, the global economic and financial crisis that resulted in the Euro crisis. This global financial crisis began with a credit-financed real-estate bubble in the United States. Its bursting had dragged the American financial system into the abyss. Between 2008 and 2012, no fewer than 465 American banks went bankrupt.

The US financial system was in ruins. But just a few years later, it looked like the Eurozone was the big loser of the crisis, not the US: the Eurozone's gross domestic product needed more than half a decade, until 2015, to return to pre-crisis levels. In the US, the country where the crisis started, it was already a good 10 percent above the pre-crisis level at the same time. At the beginning of the 2010s, the EU and US economies were quite close in size, with a size difference of just over 10 percent. By 2015 this difference had risen to almost 6,000 billion. Today, at market prices, the US economy is almost twice the size of the European economy.

The Eurozone has lost significant ground to the US economy over the last decade, particularly during crises. That brings me to my central point: lack of crisis competence is extremely expensive. In the words of Martina Navratilova, the best tennis player in the world for a long time: "To get ahead and stay there, it's not how good you are when you're good, it's how good you are when you're bad."[5]

Developing crisis competence represents a particular challenge for Germany. Our specialty is formulating rules to avoid crises, not dealing with crises. Restraint instead of actionism, stable framework conditions instead of direct intervention, rules instead of experiments—these are the foundations of economic policy in the Federal Republic of Germany. Rule orientation occupies a prominent position in German economic policy thinking, especially in international comparison.

The state sets and protects this regulatory framework within which competition, innovation, and growth can take place, but it does not otherwise interfere further. As a referee, it neither intervenes in the game of market forces nor changes the rules too often. The state relies on constancy. This rule-based thinking has its historical roots not least in the dissociation from the Nazi era, when the National Socialists made the state the instrument of a dictatorial takeover of the economy and society.

But the perception of the Weimar Republic also played an important role. The Weimar state was perceived as a plaything of economic interests, as a crisis-ridden, interventionist state overburdened with tasks and ultimately weak, which led to the state crisis. This overloading of tasks, which had contributed to the crisis at the end of the Weimar Republic, was not to be repeated.

While Carl Schmitt welcomed the crisis and the state of emergency and described it as a moment in which it became apparent who was sovereign, the avoidance of the state of emergency was from then on at the center of liberal thinking in Germany.

But there is also another reading of the crisis of the 1930s. Many countries were in crisis during the Great Depression; it was a global phenomenon that affected all countries. Some coped with it: the US under President Franklin D. Roosevelt, but also the Netherlands and the United Kingdom managed to get out of this global crisis. Germany did not. Reich Chancellor Heinrich Brüning and others deliberately exacerbated the economic crisis and overstretched the system politically and economically, even when the cracks could no longer be overlooked. What was lacking was the ability and the will to change course, the ability to do differently today what was thought to be right yesterday. The "Hunger Chancellor" stayed the course, but in the end the patient was dead.

There is no question that economic policy rules are important; they structure and maintain the normal state of affairs. They help avoid crises. Think, for example, of the much-discussed debt brake, a rule that is supposed to prevent us from getting into a crisis. But when it comes to crisis management and conflicting goals between short-term stabilization and long-term order, other perspectives and options for action become important. While in normal times the motto is that no government control is the best control, this does not necessarily apply in moments of crisis.

In crises, quick, decisive action is required. Improvisation and sometimes unconventional solutions become important. It's about leadership. It's about making decisions for which there is no rule book, where unexpected risks have to be pragmatically assessed, and where speed and the ability to get things roughly right are more important than thoroughness and exact adherence to the rules.

This requires self-confidence, flexibility in thinking, the willingness to rethink the tried and tested and throw overboard rules that stand in your way, and the realization that in crisis management sometimes things are necessary that are wrong in normal times. Such switching between normal and exceptional states is a necessary prerequisite for success in crises. It requires structures and processes with which options for action can be generated in real time, and in which science and politics come together.

"*Tempora mutantur nos et mutamur in illis.*" You may remember this beautiful hexameter by Ovid from Latin class. "The times change and we change with them." The turning point, the sudden awakening in another world, is the modern version of this old Latin phrase.

Germany must now quickly build the intellectual infrastructure to overcome this polycrisis. Here too, the experience of the last few years is central for me. We have seen that we lack the structures necessary to manage crises that encompass economic, foreign policy, and security policy issues.

We are not well prepared for what lies ahead. Last but not least, rapid government coordination is crucial in crisis situations. Without an efficient and crisis-proof state, we will not be able to overcome the crises. State capacity is a central task for the future in which we must invest. Where this is lacking and when science is left out, it is special interests and lobby groups that fill the intellectual vacuum with their arguments. This is certainly not the way to get through the polycrisis.

In the future, more than ever before, we will need the ability to deal with these shocks and difficulties. In this respect, the wisdom of German soccer player and manager Sepp Herberger also applies here in a modified form: after the crisis is before the crisis.[6]

Notes

1. This article is a slightly re-worked version of a lecture given at the Convoco! Forum on July 29, 2023 in Salzburg.

2. Adam Tooze, "Welcome to the World of Polycrisis," *Financial Times*, October 28, 2023, https://www.ft.com/content/498398e7-11b1-494b-9cd3-6d669dc3de33, (accessed November 21, 2023).

3. Bruno Latour, "Is this a Dress Rehearsal?", *Critical Inquiry*, 47 (2021), p. 2, https://www.journals.uchicago.edu/doi/full/10.1086/711428, (accessed November 21, 2023).

4. Federal Ministry for Economic Affairs and Energy, "Digitalisierung in Deutschland – Lehren aus der Corona-Krise," March 12, 2021, p. 21, https://www.bmwk.de/Redaktion/DE/Publikationen/Ministerium/Veroeffentlichung-Wissenschaftlicher-Beirat/gutachten-digitalisierung-in-deutschland.pdf?__blob=publicationFile, (accessed November 21, 2023).

5. "What matters isn't how well you play when you're playing well. What matters is how well you play when you're playing badly." Clive James, "The Champion Talkers," BBC News, July 13, 2007, http://news.bbc.co.uk/1/hi/magazine/6897462.stm, (accessed November 21, 2023).

6. "Nach dem Spiel ist vor dem Spiel" ("After the match is before the match"), 1954.

CHAPTER 2

THE CASE OF EMERGENCY AS A CRISIS OF GOVERNANCE AND LEGITIMATION: A HISTORICAL PERSPECTIVE

JÖRN LEONHARD

"Only human beings can recognize catastrophes, provided they survive them; nature recognizes no catastrophes." Max Frisch's assertion, which appears in his 1979 novella *Man in the Holocene*, refers to how a crisis event is perceived and interpreted. In this respect, the "case of emergency" does not represent an objective fact from the outset; rather, it requires people to be aware of the crisis and the subsequent interpretation and categorization of such experiences.

If we take revolutions and wars as paradigmatic examples of "cases of emergency," in modern history they have repeatedly tested the efficiency of political and social systems. The result might be legitimation crises, which could lead to the erosion of a system, or to the state, society, and economy speeding up their processes of adaptation.

I. THE "CASE OF EMERGENCY" IN HISTORY: SYSTEMIC AND LEGITIMATION CRISES IN MODERN TIMES

In these terms, the consequences of wars in particular went far beyond the immediate results of purely military conflicts. Especially in more protracted wars that incurred enormous costs and casualties, experiences contradicted the rhetorical promises of "victories" and "breakthroughs" with which wars had often begun. In modern times the experience of war included a lack of plans or indeed blueprints for many problems such as supplying both the fighting front and home front, financing lengthy campaigns, and the equitable distribution of sacrifices and burdens. In the case of emergency of an unforeseeably long war, many pre-war plans had to be discarded due to unplanned events, contingent processes, and the need for improvisation. In the absence of quick and decisive battles, many wartime societies adopted an attitude of endurance and perseverance. In this respect, wars in particular have repeatedly revealed the dysfunctional nature of political or economic structures and the limits of planning.

Against this backdrop, major crisis events such as wars and revolutions offer test cases for the management abilities of politics, economics, and society. This is true for the state during the French Revolution and in the global economic crisis of the late 1920s, as well as for the social security systems during both world wars and at the end of *Les Trente Glorieuses*—in the post-boom period of the 1970s. Although the crisis was perceived as dramatic, concrete options for action often appeared very limited. At this point an important basic pattern of cases of emergency in history emerged: every crisis that broke out—a major war or a revolution—differed from the development that had been prophesied, planned, and forecast. As wars or revolutions lasted ever longer, unanticipated events, and with them the pressure on political and social systems, increased significantly. The course of World War I was an example of this constellation. Following the summer of 1914, an ever-widening gap arose between detailed military planning and a lack of preparation for an unpredictably long war. This resulted in huge problems when it came to supplying the troops with munitions and in a serious crisis of raw materials in the German Reich, to which only Walther Rathenau found a solution through a system of state management and the production of substitute raw materials. Another reaction saw the development of structures of "organized capitalism" in which the war-state brought in corporatist mechanisms to mediate between the interests of companies and unions so that the home front pulled together.

How war operated as a "major case of emergency" in modern societies, as a test case for state action, could be seen in the close relationship between wars, nation-building, and political participation that emerged since the 16th century. Since the Early Modern period, the war-state and the fiscal state formed two sides of the same coin within the "fiscal-military state." In addition, in order to ensure a minimum degree of trust in state financial policy ("no taxation without representation"), the concept of the fiscal state and statutory participation were linked by institutionally involving those subject to tax in political decisions. After 1815 the former member states of Napoleon's Confederation of the Rhine demonstrated how national debt could operate as a powerful catalyst for reform agendas in times of war. This effect of war also continued into the 20th century, when the experiences of both world wars acted as a catalyst in creating the structures of the welfare state—the welfare programs of the Weimar Republic as well as Britain's public health system after 1945.

The connection between wartime defeats and impetus for reform also belongs in this context where the effect of wars as a case of emergency impacts the management abilities of politics, economics, and society. Wars have repeatedly acted as historical tests of efficiency, not just in terms of military performance, but also in terms of the credibility and thus the future viability of political and social structures. Against this backdrop, Prussia's post-1806 reforms were an attempt initiated by reformist civil servants and progressive military officers to find an answer to Prussia's catastrophic defeat at the hands of Napoleon. Russia's defeat in the Crimean War of 1856 intensified efforts to implement sweeping reforms in the Tsarist Empire, and it was only the defeat against Japan in 1905 that transformed the autocratic monarchy of the Tsars, at least on a formal level, into a constitutional monarchy with a parliament. The fact that such a systemic reform did not happen in 1917 after a series of military defeats would contribute significantly to the success of the Bolsheviks. Equally, the "Austro-Hungarian compromise" enacted in the Habsburg Monarchy in 1867 followed on from a military defeat. The solution to the German question in favor of Prussia as a result of the Battle of Königgrätz in 1866 forced the Viennese government to set its own monarchy within a new constitutional framework. The domestic reform agenda of France's Third Republic also owed much to the trauma of defeat in 1870/71. In these cases, internal regeneration alongside the willingness to learn from one's enemy always seemed to be a decisive precondition for aggression abroad in the future. Things were different in the case of the catastrophic defeats suffered by Germany and Japan in 1945, when the outcome of the war marked the end of a fascist or military-autocratic regime. Over the long term, this gave them a head start in the process of fresh political beginnings and socio-economic recovery. After 1945 factors that had long been a burden on West Germany disappeared, particularly the military as a "state within a state," but also the role of agrarian elites in politics.

At the same time, wars served as a test of political, social, and economic resilience—and thus of systemic legitimation. For example, World War I demonstrated the long-term superiority of more democratic states over autocratic military monarchies. This was particularly evident in how the burdens of war were distributed. During a serious domestic crisis in France, which in 1917 was accompanied by mass mutinies at the front and strikes in important industrial centers, the political leaders managed to maintain a minimum of trust in political decisions and actors despite serious clashes. This also applied to Great Britain and the United States. Despite enormous burdens, politicians such as Woodrow Wilson, David Lloyd George, and George Clemenceau maintained their credibility and contributed to the integration of their wartime societies, while in fall 1918 the monarchs and most of the military leaders in the Central Powers had lost almost all trust.

The case of emergency would not only operate as a test of efficiency and an impetus for reform, it also intensified debates in the early 20th century about the nature of sovereignty. For example, Carl Schmitt's argument was based on the experience of crisis since the world war and looked primarily at the modern war-state with its new instruments, in which "organized capitalism" and the concept of *Volksgemeinschaft* [national community] that had emerged during the world war were used to negate divisions between social classes. Schmitt objected to the paradigm of sovereignty of the people and traditional natural rights and focused on the state of emergency and state of exception. In his interpretation, "sovereignty" did not come about as a result of the regular rhythm of parliamentary legislatures, but rather from a situation of crisis and the reaction to it. For Schmitt, the "sovereign" was therefore the one who could decide on a state of exception and thus define the "case of emergency" in the first place.

From this analysis of the urgent solution to a crisis, Schmitt derived a decidedly anti-democratic model of political rule. Unsurprisingly, in the crisis of democracies after 1918, an intense debate arose about the problem-solving capacity of deliberative democracy, which its opponents repeatedly accused of ultimately not being able to cope with fundamental internal and external crises. After 1917, this controversy had developed between the two poles of the Soviet (council) model on the one hand and representative democracy based on elections and parliaments on the other, before other radical alternative models emerged in the shape of Italian fascism and National Socialism.

II. "CASE OF EMERGENCY" AND "POLYCRISIS": ON SOME CONTEMPORARY INDICATORS

Against the backdrop of this historical sketch, how can we describe the present "case of emergency"? What are the specific indicators of the current crisis experience? To begin with, the category of crisis usually emerged retrospectively. The crisis-like nature of the context of events that we associate with the dates 1776 or 1789 was only revealed through knowledge of the consequences of actions and events that were not foreseeable as such either in the years 1776 or 1789 themselves. Thus the much-discussed "age of revolutions" as a way of labeling eras emerged in retrospect. In contrast to the idea of a break with the past that was intended from the outset, many revolutions did not indeed begin with the claim to be creating something completely new, but rather with the aim of restoring an ancient, apparently questioned, and often idealized system, and were therefore based on a cyclical notion of time. However, since the beginning of the 20th century there have also been times of emergency in which contemporaries were already immediately aware of the nature of the profound upheaval—the point of no return—albeit unable to assess the consequences accurately. This was true for the outbreak of

World War I in August 1914, for the escalation of World War II into Eastern Europe and the Pacific in June and December 1941, for the end of the Cold War in November 1989, the terrorist attack on the United States in September 2001, and Russia's invasion of Ukraine in February 2022.

Two characteristics in particular distinguish the present from older patterns of experience. First, there is now a global communications network that enables an unprecedented feeling of being a "contemporary eyewitness." This applies both quantitatively and qualitatively when it comes to social media, and it has, for example, massively changed the global perception of victims and experiences of violence. Social media turns globalism into a mode of constant comparison. It contributes to the emergence of competing public spheres where opinions can be mobilized at any moment. In this context, the traditional separation between domestic and foreign policy seems to be pushed increasingly into the background.

Second, we are currently dealing with an unprecedented collision of long-, medium-, and short-term crisis phenomena. Following Fernand Braudel, we might identify three levels of "temporality" in the crises that are currently converging: the *longue durée* of climate, environment, and geography; the *moyenne durée* with regard to demographics and economic cycles; and the level of évènements in immediate political decision-making processes. All three temporal levels are intertwined in the present and reinforce each other. On top of this there are the costs of the Anthropocene resulting from the twin crises of climate and biodiversity and in light of the foreseeable end of the age of fossil fuels; the demographic crisis and its implications for the future of democracy and the welfare state; digitalization and the technological change accelerated by artificial intelligence that is creating completely new opportunities and threats for political communication and social conflicts; an erosion of traditional political and social systems through the increased polarization of globalization's apparent "winners" and "losers"; and a crisis-like upheaval in the structure of the "outside" and "inside" of states and societies, with the result that the traditional context of sovereignty defined by nation states seems to be eroding, provoking even more aggressive kinds of nationalism in response.

III. OUTLOOK: A HISTORICAL PERSPECTIVE ON DEMOCRACY'S RESILIENCE AND ABILITY TO GOVERN

In light of these developments, the question of political governance and the ability to govern becomes even more urgent: so, what condition is the resilience of political and social systems in? Looking ahead, we can offer just a few final thoughts.

First, the altered nature of political communications is even more apparent than in earlier periods. This complex includes the pluralization of public spheres with their own logics of opinion-making and political mobilization, as well as an overall huge acceleration of reactions, which makes political decision-making processes seem structurally deficient. Political actors claim comprehensive problem-solving skills, and their promises to find solutions create ever-increasing expectations. In reality, however, the often-limited tools for implementation, the need to prioritize, and the often narrow scope for action lead to disappointment and disillusionment. Therefore, realistic "expectation management" becomes even more important. Behind this lies a fundamental problem in modern politics: the relationship between what can be said and what can be done. The perceived gap between these two poles is often the starting point for legitimation crises. It is the very nature of how modern media and communications work that makes it increasingly difficult to assess collective reactions realistically. This means that unintended consequences and unplanned results happen more frequently, and it is these very unintended consequences that can challenge the legitimacy of political decisions.

Second, since the late 19th century, and especially in the context of the world wars, there has been a growing awareness of the transnational nature of many political, economic, and social problems. This concerned debts and loans, refugees, minorities, and new policy areas such as health, security, and the environment. Despite these transnational challenges, the sovereign nation state has been and continues to be the frame of reference for political decision-making processes, for constitutions, elections, and parliaments, for welfare and security. Alongside this tension we see the contrast between universal promises on the one hand—from the global vocabulary of self-determination that emerged from World War I to notions of universally applicable human rights and standards for political participation and social justice—and subsidiary practices on the other. Setting local constellations and particular interests within the context of universal goals was what characterized the 1918 and 1945 postwar periods in particular as a "glocalism."

In such a constellation, is democracy, as the framework of free societies, overwhelmed and inferior in light of the pressure created by the problem? In historical periods of crisis such as wars, an equitable distribution of burdens was of crucial importance in order to maintain the credibility of a political and social system. For example, the impression of collectivizing casualties and privatizing profits during World War I led time and again to serious domestic and sociopolitical conflicts in the war-states. But contrary to the notion that autocracies can always act more successfully in wars because they do not have to take account of competing opinions or political opposition, democracies turned out to be relatively adaptable in a long and costly conflict such as World War I. France, Great Britain, and the United States were better able to learn, adapt, and manage their failures up to the end. In this way they were able to accept a minimum amount of constructive competition, even if important requirements came under increasing pressure.

The resilience of political and social systems involves confidence in the system and trust in individuals. Ideally, a political system is underpinned by a mixture of both, with institutions, processes, and actors balancing and complementing each other. For the United States to emerge from the double crisis of democracy and capitalism in the late 1920s, it was not just faith in institutions and processes that was crucial, but also the presence of credible individuals such as President Franklin D. Roosevelt with his media-friendly demeanor.

In the Netherlands, democracy survived in the 1930s for two main reasons. First, over decades the Dutch had developed a state that people trusted. This gave rise to a resilient political structure that knew how to deal with various internal and external shocks and threats. Second, the political system proved to be able to react flexibly to crises and thus create a "defensive democracy" – *avant la lettre*. Thus, the system did not have to anticipate specific threats, but was based on a mixture of proactive and reactive approaches. Third and finally, in acute crises a well-established culture of moderation came into play. From an overarching perspective, the survival of democracy depended on three interconnected factors: cleverly constructed institutions that people trusted; transparent political decisions; and moderation in the practical interactions between the system's representatives. In this example, decidedly pre-political attributes—empathy, trust, moderation, solidarity, justice, patience, the ability to compromise—were of enormous importance.

In any case, an examination of these examples from the 1920s and 1930s warns us not to assume from our present-day accumulation of crises that democracy is no longer able to meet the demands of political and social governance and that a crisis of democracy is therefore unavoidable. A case of emergency is always also an opportunity that recalls the fundamentally open meaning of "crisis"—not as a negative characterization of an event, but as a decision-making phase whose outcome is open. From a German perspective, we are basing our view of the years around 1930 on the experiences from the Weimar Republic. But by choosing a different focus—for example, on the United States, Great Britain, and the Netherlands—this historical period also contains many of the conditions needed for the resilience of democracy to mobilize and to succeed.

References

Fernand Braudel, *The Mediterranean and the Mediterranean World in the Age of Philip II*, 3 vols. (Berkeley CA: University of California Press, 1996).

Ute Frevert (ed.), *Vertrauen. Historische Annäherungen* (Göttingen: Vandenhoeck & Ruprecht, 2003).

Max Frisch, *Man in the Holocene*, trans. Geoffrey Skelton (Dallas TX: Dalkey Archive Press, 2009).

Reinhart Koselleck, "Krise," in Otto Brunner, Werner Conze, and Reinhart Koselleck (eds.), *Geschichtliche Grundbegriffe. Historisches Lexikon zur politisch-sozialen Sprache in Deutschland*, vol. 3 (Stuttgart: Klett-Cotta, 1982), pp. 617–50.

Jörn Leonhard, *Pandora's Box: A History of the First World War*, trans. Patrick Camiller (Cambridge MA/London: The Belknap Press of Harvard University Press, 2018).

Niklas Luhmann, *Trust and Power* (Cambridge: Polity, 2017).

Thomas Mergel (ed.), *Krisen verstehen. Historische und kulturwissenschaftliche Annäherungen* (Frankfurt: Campus Verlag, 2012).

Carla Meyer, Katja Patzel-Mattern, and Gerrit Jasper Schenk (eds.), *Krisengeschichte(n). "Krise" als Leitbegriff und Erzählmuster in kulturwissenschaftlicher Perspektive* (Stuttgart: Franz Steiner Verlag, 2013).

Carl Schmitt, *Political Theology: Four Chapters on the Concept of Sovereignty*, trans. George Schwab (Cambridge MA: The MIT Press, 1986).

François Walter, *Catastrophes: Une histoire culturelle (XVIe–XXIe siècle)* (Paris: Seuil, 2008).

Thomas Weber (ed.), *Als die Demokratie starb. Die Machtergreifung der Nationalsozialisten – Geschichte und Gegenwart* (Freiburg: Herder Verlag, 2022).

CHAPTER 3

IS THE WESTERN INSTITUTIONAL CONSENSUS SUSTAINABLE?

MARIETTA AUER

The history of humanity is a history of crises. Wars, civil wars, economic collapses, epidemics, crop failures, famines, migrations, and violent land grabs are not experiences that are confined to modern times. And yet there is often a sense that a period as crisis-ridden as today in the early 21st century has never existed before. The economic historian Adam Tooze talks about a "polycrisis," meaning a state of multiple crises that overlap and intensify each other, thus keeping society as a whole in the identified current state of continuous crisis.[1] And indeed, scarcely a day goes by without reports of new crises or old crises re-emerging in a new guise. The 2008 financial crisis was quickly followed by the Euro crisis, the migration crisis, the pandemic crisis, the Ukraine and energy price crisis, and now a new Middle East and migration crisis. These are always accompanied by the *basso continuo* of the overarching climate crisis and the global crisis of liberal democracies suffering under the new onslaught of competition from authoritarian systems.[2]

The world order is being put to the test. This raises the question of which systems and institutions shape our world and how resilient they are. To put it bluntly: can the Western institutional consensus withstand the current polycrisis? The following essay is devoted to this question, looking at a narrow selection of social institutions, the entirety of which is referred to here as the "Western institutional consensus." This consensus is based on five institutional pillars: the separation of state and society; liberal democracy; the Westphalian system of sovereign states; the capitalist market system; and an informal moral consensus regarding the basic conditions of coexistence in a society structured in this way. These five elements make up the institutional framework of the Western world and are crucial for its normative self-image. Whether the Western institutional consensus can withstand the multiple crises of the 21st century depends on the interaction between all these elements as well as on the resilience of each individual pillar.

I. WHAT ARE INSTITUTIONS?

First, however, the concept of "institution" needs further clarification. What do we mean when we talk about "institutions"? The term is used in all the social sciences but does not always mean the same thing. Sociologists talk about institutions when they are describing self-organizing systems of social control. In economics, the focus is on institutionally created structures that incentivize individual or collective action. A functional definition emphasizes the way institutions facilitate social interaction. Phenomenologically, we can distinguish between different levels in the overall institutional structure of society, such as the informal rules of tradition, *Weltanschauung*, and culture, as against the formal rules of law and the economic system of resource allocation and behavior control through contracts.[3] Regardless of which definition we look at in detail, two aspects are essential. On the one hand, the way institutions facilitate social interaction as mentioned above, which makes institutions an indispensable and ubiquitous part of social interactions. Without institutions, we literally couldn't step outside our front door because there is no aspect of human coexistence that is not institutionally regulated—for this reason alone we should take an interest in the resilience of institutions in the event of a crisis. On the other hand, their ubiquity once again emphasizes the importance of informal institutions—whether cultural, familial, social, moral, or religious—without which complex formal institutions such as the legal system or the constitution of democratic politics would lose their cohesion and meaning.

Then again, the ubiquitous significance of institutions also emphasizes the danger of institutional totalitarianism.[4] Totalitarian institutions characterize not only authoritarian states, but also authoritarian systems of belief and morality. The Western institutional consensus was created precisely to curb religious totalitarianism. It arose against the background of the European wars of religion in the Enlightenment period between 1650 and 1800. It is expressed paradigmatically in Immanuel Kant's dream of "perpetual peace." This sees the problem of establishing a state as resolvable even for a "race of devils" if they would only use their reason to transform their conflicting egoisms into a peaceful national constitution through general laws created in the interest of the greater whole—the advantages of which would benefit every individual as a peace dividend.[5] In this sense, the liberal thinking of the Enlightenment aims to form institutions so that they provide the individual with support and guidance, but still leave them free to re-shape these institutions according to their needs, thus avoiding institutional totalitarianism. This applies on both a small and a large scale to the informal institutions of everyday coexistence just as much as to the political and international institutions of state organization.

But this fundamental idea does not go unchallenged. The Western institutional consensus has been threatened with dangers for some time now, not only from outside, but also and especially from within, due to the collapse of its own value base. Against this backdrop, the current polycrisis is ultimately just the latest escalation of a long-identified crisis of Enlightenment thought that is posing a radical challenge to the Western model of society.[6] What this means to each individual building block of the Western institutional consensus is considered below.

II. STATE VERSUS SOCIETY

The first of these building blocks is the institutional separation of state and society, the flipside of which is that both parties nevertheless remain inextricably linked to one another in their claim to legitimacy. The separation of state and society expresses a fundamental principle of the anti-totalitarian consensus of Enlightenment thought. In this world view, the state has a necessarily limited task.[7] It derives its legitimacy from society; it exists for society and not society for the state. Society exists autonomously from the state; the free activity of its members is guaranteed by liberal fundamental and human rights and protected from state intervention. The freedom that prevails in society can also be described as negative freedom or freedom from external coercion.[8] In the liberal institutional consensus, the state has no power to prescribe how its members exercise their freedom and, for example, to tell them how they should lead their lives. In this world view, the only legitimate way to exercise political power is the democratic decision-making process, in which the members of society join together as citizens in democratic institutions in order to give themselves general laws for living together in society according to democratic procedural rules. The dualism of state and society is thus reflected in a corresponding dualism of the roles of the individual in the state or in society. In the state, the individual as a *citoyen* is under the law an equal political citizen and political decision-maker; in society, by contrast, as a *bourgeois* addressee of freedom, the individual is protected against state interference in their discretionary exercise of freedom. It is characteristic of the Enlightenment worldview that the potential contradiction between the individual's two roles is in theory minimized or even completely ignored: it did not occur to the philosophers of the Enlightenment that citizens, as private individuals, could think and act in anything other than a statesmanlike way.[9]

However, it is precisely this rift between private and public interests that in reality cannot be suppressed which causes the central problem of legitimacy in the liberal social constitution. For Hegel, this is the irresolvable contradiction between the particularity of individual freedom and the universality of the state as a whole, which drives civil society to constantly overreach itself and at the same time leads to the erosion of its inner substance.[10] Karl Marx turns the thrust of this criticism against the Enlightenment constitution of civil society itself and argues that the state guarantee of social emancipation through liberal basic rights actually serves the perpetuation of social power and inequality.[11] This criticism was repeated and taken up many times during the 19th and 20th centuries. Since then, the tenor of this criticism has been, in many different versions, that there is no such thing as a society that is autonomous from the state, rather that state and society are inextricably linked. The state often intervenes in society to regulate it and does not have a neutral attitude towards it. The balance of legitimacy between state and society accepted by the liberal thinkers of the Enlightenment period was based from the outset on an illusion that could never be realistically achieved in Western societies.

Nevertheless, as long as the state was able to fulfill its democratically legitimate normative role in a liberal society smoothly, it was possible to exclude it from the liberal model of society, at least theoretically. What is new is that for some time now this theoretical option has been faltering under shifts in the overall structure of the liberal institutional consensus. New problems arise that no longer fit with the old worldview. These include global challenges such as climate change and global crises of migration and poverty that overwhelm the state's socially limited range of control and are experienced in Western societies as a critical failure of management. This management crisis is exacerbated by the regulatory failure of an increasingly micro-managing legal system, whose response to its own powerlessness when dealing with global polycrises is a flood of new regulations, which it in turn increasingly fails to enforce, thus further undermining its own legitimacy.[12] All of this does not go unnoticed by society. The consequence of the management failures that are experienced every day is a gradual but sustained loss of trust in state institutions. But once trust is lost, it is hard to restore. The consequences for the liberal institutional consensus are incalculable.

III. LIBERAL DEMOCRACY

Let us take a closer look at the state institutions we have just discussed. In keeping with the Western institutional consensus, they are democratically constituted. This means that institutions such as parliaments, courts, and administrative authorities are founded on democratic principles and operate according to democratic rules of procedure. Once again, this institutional design is a consequence of the Enlightenment credo that totalitarian institutional power is always illegitimate. Institutional power can only be justified if those affected by it consent to it freely and are always able to revoke this consent. In this regard, the principle of democracy represents the notion of collective autonomy: decisions that affect a large number of people are only legitimate if they are supported by the collective self-determination of all those involved. In constitutional practice, the principle of democracy is implemented primarily through parliamentary legislative procedures, whose institutional legitimacy results from the fact that they guarantee the procedural participation in the democratic process of all those subject to the law.

But here too the liberal institutional consensus is increasingly running into difficulties. In and of itself, democracy—despite early and often repeated warnings about its degeneration into modern forms of mass dictatorship[13]—is perfectly designed to balance conflicting interests, values, and opinions through its political procedures. However, it is now becoming apparent that there are fundamental issues regarding community life about which consensus on shared values and interests can no longer be reached. This is where a flaw in the liberal institutional consensus becomes apparent, which, after Amartya Sen, has been aptly called the "liberal paradox."[14] Liberal democracies have no overarching decision-making rule to create a consensus on the subject of the political consensus, i.e., on what can be negotiated politically at all, by contrast with what at least a vocal minority claims as sacrosanct or out of the question. It is therefore no accident that today's public discourse is characterized by problems such as "how much freedom should the enemies of freedom be given?" The fragmentation of Western societies is often bemoaned, resulting in the claim that their ideological polarization is reaching the point where political action is impossible, paired with the diagnosis of emerging parallel societies that no longer share a common value base.[15] Hand in hand with this goes a domestic political trend towards a new kind of authoritarianism. Even in the wealthy Western countries (or especially there) moderate political movements are getting left behind while the extremes are gaining strength. For some observers, the historically proven risk that democratic systems can abandon the center ground, tip over into totalitarianism, and be overrun by authoritarian regimes is now once more close at hand. Some even point to the 1920s as a reflection of today's situation.[16]

In addition, extra-democratic systemic competition is becoming evident not only inside but also outside the community of Western states. One look at China, Russia, Turkey, or the Middle East is enough to see how precarious and contested the island of liberal democracies has become in today's world. The prematurely announced "end of history" has long since been abandoned.[17] In global terms, today those voices who are indifferent, dismissive, or even openly hostile to liberal democracy based on the Western model are in the majority.

IV. THE WESTPHALIAN SYSTEM

A corollary to the democratically constituted state system is the Westphalian system of sovereign states, whose name refers to the 1648 Peace of Westphalia, albeit without any claim to historical accuracy. This term describes the international order that emerged in modern Europe and is still valid today, based on a system in which equal, sovereign states are the exclusive actors in international law and international politics. States are also the exclusive actors in legitimate warfare. Moreover, the Westphalian system reflects the fundamental liberal ideas of Enlightenment thought. For example, the principles of sovereignty and territoriality, according to which every state is sovereign domestically and externally and defined by fixed borders, derive from the same collective notion of autonomy or right to self-determination of the peoples that laid the foundations of modern nation states. This was originally a liberal idea, as was the abolition of religion as the defining principle of the international legal system since the 1555 Peace of Augsburg. Added to this is the Westphalian system's principle of legality, which binds all sovereign states to international law based on voluntarily concluded treaties, and thus does not rely on any superior power.

However, the notion of sovereign nation states as the foundations of an equal and legitimate international system has also been criticized for some time. The system, which has been parodied as the "Westfailure system," is accused of a very lack of sovereignty in the face of the coequal capitalist economic system, and of therefore systematically failing to deal with major crises such as the Asian financial crisis of 1997 and 1998, the climate crisis, or the growing global inequality crisis.[18] In other respects too the idea that state sovereignty expresses the collective right to self-determination of the peoples represented by the state and empowers them to enjoy equal representation under international law has lost its legitimacy. Under pressure from post-national and post-colonial movements, a post-Western world order has emerged that dismisses as ideological the West's understanding of the formal equality and international legality of sovereign states in a world that is still characterized by colonial imbalances. In the post-Westphalian world order, new ideologies are now dominant, including asymmetrical forms of war and terrorism, which push the sanctions mechanisms of classical international law to their limits.[19] The outlook for the Westphalian system is a new reality of internationally uncontrollable violent conflicts.

V. CAPITALISM AND PRIVATE LAW

The counterpart of the Western state system based on liberalism, democracy, and sovereignty is a model of society based on individual autonomy, the market, competition, and the capitalist economy. The fundamental institutional framework of such a social system is guaranteed by private law, which provides organizational forms and allocative rights such as property, contract, and corporations that are fundamental to capitalist economic structures.[20] Above all, the invention of the modern corporation, which began with the founding of the East India Companies in Europe from 1600, provided a legal and institutional boost to innovation, which formed the basis for the development of industrial capitalism in England and Scotland from the 18th century onwards. By the 19th century, however, the capitalist economy's serious potential for inequality was recognized and was being debated as the "social question." Karl Marx's aforementioned criticism of civil society and its constitutionally guaranteed freedom to administer unequal treatment also addresses this question.[21] The 20th century reacted to these early symptoms of crisis in the global capitalist economy by developing models of state regulation as applied to markets and working conditions that differed considerably from country to country. The Rhenish model of consensus-based capitalism that predominates in Germany, perfected in the years post-1945, is fundamentally different from Anglo-Saxon, Scandinavian, and Asian economic cultures. It relies on the institutionalized consensus of social partnership, the purpose of which is to resolve class antagonisms corporately and thus forestall them from the outset through institutional integration—a striking example of the political benefits of integrative institutions.[22]

However, in the 1970s and 1980s the various models of regulated capitalism cushioned by welfare-state or corporate institutions entered a global crisis. Since then, due to the effects of shrinking economic growth, rising inflation, and persistent unemployment in the Western industrialized nations, economic policy corrections have taken place to wind down welfare-state institutions, privatize public services, reduce trade union influence, and withdraw state redistribution policies. This paradigm shift towards a neo-liberalization of global market activity is known generally as "Reaganomics" and "Thatcherism." It may not so much have deepened the global divide between rich and poor—which can arguably be contested by the fact that new participation in the markets of the Global North has enabled growth above average in many cases, especially in the Global South, and has contributed to the emergence of a new middle class— but rather has created new strata of "social losers" in the capitalist economies of the Global North themselves. Even among the academically qualified middle classes such strata have emerged—marginalized groups that have since become a threat to the stability of Western democracies.[23] The most recent crises have exacerbated these effects globally. Since then, hardly a day has gone by without the appearance of a new publication on the global legitimacy crisis of capitalism and the political explosiveness of the increasing gap between rich and poor.[24] It is as if the social consensus, still in existence until the turn of the millennium, that even major differences in wealth are acceptable if they benefit everyone by making economic growth, redistribution, and social security affordable, had suddenly disappeared. The slogan of the Occupy Wall Street movement of 2011, "We are the 99%," anticipates the mood of this new global class struggle.[25]

VI. ETHICAL LIFE AND INTEGRATION

The above has been considering the social consensus that underpins the legitimacy of the private economy. However, this is just one example of the multitude of unwritten institutions, i.e., generally shared social norms, rules, and patterns of behavior, on which the stability of the Western institutional consensus is largely based. This refers to unwritten rules of social behavior and institutional expectations. They concern, for example, the level of individual responsibility for maintaining society as a whole, the existence of a fundamental consensus on the demarcation line between the public and private spheres, trust in state institutions, or the rules of discourse that apply in public debate. Until the 19th century such unwritten laws of social intercourse were discussed under the heading of "ethical life" [*Sittlichkeit*]—already with the feeling that they were being eroded by the loss of solidarity caused by the selfishness of modern society.[26] In the 20th century, the sociologists' term "integration" replaced this. The notion of "integration" is still used to describe this political problem: how can the diverging wills of individual members of society be translated into a community-spirited civil society under the liberal premise that the exercise of individual freedom does not require public justification? The unwritten institutional foundations of liberal society thus turn out to be the main battlefield for its aforementioned normative paradox. In practice this manifests itself as a delicate balance being constantly renegotiated between the liberal credo that individual freedom is exempt from public justification and the constant challenge to this consensus by an increasingly fragmented society—a society whose integration through shared values or some other unifying whole is becoming increasingly unlikely.[27]

The constitutional lawyer Ernst-Wolfgang Böckenförde summed up this paradox of liberal society in a much-quoted dictum, the so-called Böckenförde dictum: "The liberal, secularized state lives by prerequisites which it cannot guarantee itself."[28] Unlike the ideal assumption of the Western liberal fundamental consensus, the spheres of culture, religion, and ethical life—including marriage, family, sexuality, and child-rearing—cannot be seamlessly ousted from the political sphere and relegated to the private sphere as issues only concerning the private exercise of freedom.

An even more pointed version of this fundamental dilemma of legitimacy in liberal society is provided by the aforementioned "liberal paradox" in Amartya Sen's version, the basic notion of which can be summarized as follows:[29] one person's private freedom is another person's public nuisance. As a social theory, liberalism is structurally unable to formulate a definition of the minimum consensus on ethical life that is required to maintain liberalism's own conditions of existence. Liberal theorists who have nevertheless attempted such a definition—from the English and American "Cold War Liberals" of the 1940s and 1950s, who formulated their "liberalism of fear" in the shadow of the nuclear threat posed by Soviet systemic competition, to Dolf Sternberger's "constitutional patriotism," to the recurring "core culture" [*Leitkultur*] debates of today's culturally diverse societies, which are uncertain of their pluralistic existential conditions[30]— quickly acquire the reputation of being conservative, if not downright reactionary. And yet the liberal paradox will not disappear by denying it, canceling it, or otherwise excluding it from the debate about the existential conditions of the Western institutional consensus. We can of course go on behaving as if there were a sound consensus on commonly shared values that will guarantee the existence of the liberal social model into the future. However, we can no longer overlook the fact that the fundamental liberal freedoms that were fought for in lengthy political disputes to protect the exercise of private freedoms against the totalitarianism of the state are now often turned into their opposite as a cover for new social totalitarianisms in the form of religious, ethnic, and nationalist ideologies of power. A responsible kind of politics would have to take seriously the mantra "Never again!", which was the basis for the establishment of Germany after 1945, with a continual reminder that the liberal separation of ethical life and autonomy cannot be maintained. Individual and political autonomy, the crucial pillars of the liberal model of society, are only possible within a general climate of societal liberalism that consistently defends itself against new forms of totalitarianism.

Notes

1. Adam Tooze, "Welcome to the World of the Polycrisis," *Financial Times*, October 28, 2022, https://www.ft.com/content/498398e7-11b1-494b-9cd3-6d669dc3de33 (accessed May 13, 2024).

2. Christian Breuer, "Polykrise als Gefangenendilemma" in *Wirtschaftsdienst*, 103 (1) 2023, https://www.wirtschaftsdienst.eu/inhalt/jahr/2023/heft/1/beitrag/polykrise-als-gefangenendilemma.html (accessed December 12, 2023).

3. See generally Mary Douglas, *How Institutions Think* (Syracuse: Syracuse University Press, 1986).

4. See, in particular, Hannah Arendt, *The Origins of Totalitarianism* (New York: Schocken Books, 1951).

5. Immanuel Kant, *Perpetual Peace: A Philosophical Sketch*, https://www.gutenberg.org/files/50922/50922-h/50922-h.htm (accessed January 7, 2023). The third verse of Luther's hymn, *A Mighty Fortress is our God*, refers to this "race of devils":

   "And though this world, with devils filled,/
   should threaten to undo us,/
   we will not fear, for God has willed/
   his truth to triumph through us."

6. For an in-depth analysis, see Samuel Moyn, *Liberalism Against Itself: Cold War Intellectuals and the Making of Our Times* (New Haven: Yale University Press, 2023).

7. A paradigmatic work is John Locke, *Two Treatises of Government, Second Treatise* (1690), ed. Peter Laslett (Cambridge: Cambridge University Press, 1988).

8. Isaiah Berlin, "Two Concepts of Liberty" in *Four Essays on Liberty*, ed. Isaiah Berlin (Oxford: Oxford University Press, 1969), pp. 15–22.

9. See Jürgen Habermas, *The Philosophical Discourse of Modernity: Twelve Lectures*, trans. Frederick Lawrence (Cambridge: Polity Press, 1987), pp. 19 ff.

10. Georg Wilhelm Friedrich Hegel, *Elements of the Philosophy of Right* (1821), trans. H.B. Nisbet, ed. Allen W. Wood (Cambridge: Cambridge University Press, 1991), §§ 182 ff., pp. 220 ff.

11. Karl Marx, "On the Jewish Question" (1843) in Karl Marx, *Early Writings*, trans. Rodney Livingstone and Gregor Benton (Harmondsworth: Penguin 1975), pp. 211–241.

12. See Wolfgang Schön, "Deutschland steht vor dem Regulierungsbankrott" in *Frankfurter Allgemeine Zeitung*, June 27, 2023, https://www.faz.net/aktuell/wirtschaft/mehr-wirtschaft/fachkraeftemangel-und-ueberforderung-steigen-buerokratie-in-deutschland-18983064.html (accessed December 12, 2023).

13. Cf. Arendt, *The Origins of Totalitarianism*.

14. Amartya Sen, "The Impossibility of a Paretian Liberal" in *Journal of Political Economy*, 78 (1), 1970, pp. 152–57.

15. Of the many more recent publications on this topic, see Carolin Amlinger and Oliver Nachtwey, *Gekränkte Freiheit. Aspekte des libertären Autoritarismus* (Berlin: Suhrkamp, 2022); Steffen Mau, Thomas Lux, and Linus Westheuser, *Triggerpunkte: Konsens und Konflikt in der Gegenwartsgesellschaft* (Berlin: Suhrkamp, 2023).

16. For a recent example, see Benedikt Wintgens, "Weimarer Verhältnisse?" in *Frankfurter Allgemeine Zeitung*, December 11, 2023, p. 6.

17. See Francis Fukuyama, *The End of History and the Last Man* (Penguin: New York, 1992).

18. Susan Strange, "The Westfailure System" in *Review of International Studies*, 25 (3), 1999, pp. 345–54; and following this, for example: Randall Germain (ed.), *Susan Strange and the Future of Global Political Economy: Power, Control and Transformation* (London: Routledge, 2016).

19. See Herfried Münkler, *Die neuen Kriege* (Hamburg: Rowohlt, 2002).

20. On the resulting "private law society" [*Privatrechtsgesellschaft*], see Franz Böhm, "Privatrechtsgesellschaft und Marktwirtschaft" in *ORDO* 17 (1966), pp. 75–151, 121 ff.

21. Cf. Marx, "On the Jewish Question."

22. See generally James Fulcher, *Capitalism: A Very Short Introduction* (Oxford: Oxford University Press, 2016).

23. On the development of incomes globally, see Christoph Lakner and Branko Milanovic, "Global Income Distribution: From the Fall of the Berlin Wall to the Great Recession" in *Worldbank*, December 2013, https://openknowledge.worldbank.org/handle/10986/16935 (accessed December 12, 2023).

24. See Katharina Pistor, *The Code of Capital: How the Law Creates Wealth and Inequality* (Princeton: Princeton University Press, 2019).

25. See, for example, Daniel Indiviglio, "Most Americans Aren't Occupy Wall Street's '99 Percent'" in *The Atlantic*, May 10, 2011, https://www.theatlantic.com/business/archive/2011/10/most-americans-arent-occupy-wall-streets-99-percent/246196 (accessed December 12, 2023).

26. See Hegel, *Elements of the Philosophy of Right*, §§ 142 ff., pp. 187 ff.

27. See Andreas Reckwitz, *Die Gesellschaft der Singularitäten* (Berlin: Suhrkamp, 2017).

28. Ernst-Wolfgang Böckenförde, "Die Entstehung des Staates als Vorgang der Säkularisation" in Ernst-Wolfgang Böckenförde, *Recht, Staat, Freiheit: Studien zur Rechtsphilosophie, Staatstheorie und Verfassungsgeschichte* (Frankfurt am Main: Suhrkamp, 1991), pp. 92–114, 112.

29. Cf. Sen, "The Impossibility of a Paretian Liberal."

30. On "Cold War Liberalism": Moyn, *Liberalism Against Itself*; on the German debates: Dolf Sternberger, "Unvergleichlich lebensvoll, aber stets gefährdet: Ist unsere Verfassung nicht demokratisch genug?" in *Frankfurter Allgemeine Zeitung*, January 27, 1970; Daniel Thym, "Verfassungspatriotismus in der Einwanderungsgesellschaft" in *Archiv des öffentlichen Rechts*, 145 (1), 2020, pp. 40–74.

CHAPTER 4

PERHAPS IT IS TIME TO STOP THINKING IN TERMS OF THE WEST

TIM CRANE

Today we are faced with multiple crises: crises in finance and in the economy, crises of democratic legitimacy, crises of populism, the crises brought about by intractable wars. Then there is also, perhaps most fundamentally, the climate crisis. These issues are very difficult and complex to understand theoretically, but they are also of the greatest practical significance. As a philosopher, there is little I can add to the empirical, scientific, or historical understanding of these crises. In a sense philosophers must follow Socrates—"all I know is that I know nothing"—but nonetheless I believe it is still possible to offer some philosophical observations on aspects of the current situation.

The first question we are faced with is how *we* can do anything about these crises. By "we," I mean primarily thinkers: intellectuals, economists, historians, philosophers, and scientists. What can we do to address the crises? It is very natural to feel powerless and impotent in the face of some of these things. But if we are to address them, we first have to understand them. And understanding is partly a matter of trying to clarify and identify the different parts of these phenomena.

In order to do that, we need to do two things. The first is that we need to address these questions dispassionately; we need to have a sense of perspective. We need to make sure that our contributions are not parochial—by which I mean that we are not just generalizing from our own individual, local situations. I was born in 1962, and so I have lived through a period of unprecedented peace in Europe for most of its inhabitants (with the tragic exceptions of Yugoslavia, Northern Ireland, and Ukraine). It is reasonable to say that the history of Europe before that period was a long, protracted history of war. I feel very fortunate to have lived through what must have been the most peaceful period of European history.

It might feel natural to generalize from this a kind of a teleology or progress—a movement towards something. And some people have thought like this. When the Cold War ended, they conjectured that we would never return to the previous struggles. This was "the end of history," in Francis Fukuyama's phrase: the point at which our political progress had been aiming. We had arrived at our destination.

Looking back, it is clear that this was a narrow and parochial view. This is not just because during this period there were many wars going on elsewhere in the world, outside Europe. It is also because as things started to collapse in various ways, we saw that a lot of our apparent progress was illusory. The crises we experience now are the result, and they require their own understanding. Historians like Jörn Leonhard rightly tell us that there has never really been a period without crisis.[1] But that doesn't mean that all crises are the same, or that there's no reason to consider the individual crises we have now.

This brings me to the second thing that we can do as intellectuals or thinkers: we need to break these problems down into their parts. Adam Tooze's concept of "polycrisis" is a nice catchword to sum up our situation, but it's not a good explanatory tool. It doesn't help to explain what's special about the different situations, the different crises. We are facing many different problems, and they need different, individual explanations.

Combining these two points, then, gives us our starting point: we need to start with a sense of perspective, and then break down the individual problems. With that said, I'd like to make four small points with regards to Convoco's question, "Are the systems sustainable in case of emergency?" The first is about the idea of a system and of a global world order, the second about the values that systems are supposed to embody, the third is about the climate crisis, and the fourth about the concept of truth or fact.

First, I think Corinne Flick is right to argue that we're entering a period of history where things are not going to be the same.[2] I believe that there are plausible reasons to think that the systems that we're talking about, the rule-governed systems which were part of the postwar consensus, are in many ways ineffective, and some may even soon have had their day. Maybe the whole idea of "the West"—insofar as that idea is embodied in systems such as the United Nations and the World Bank and so on—has had its day too. Maybe we should stop thinking in terms of the West. Maybe there are too many differences between the different parts of the West. If Donald Trump is elected

President of the United States for a second term, and if he takes the United States further away from the path that it had been set on, then there will be even less in common between what's happening in Europe and what's happening in the United States. Maybe recognizing this will even be a good thing for the "systems" in question. Maybe we shouldn't place too much faith in these systems, and instead think of other ways in which to tackle the crises.

This brings me to my second point. I think it would be a mistake to think that the values which we associate with Western liberal democracies are necessarily dependent on having systems like this. These values, including equality and freedom (freedom of speech, freedom of the press, freedom of thought, democracy, maybe even free trade), are independent of particular structures. That should be obvious, but I think it needs to be said. The fact that the systems are under threat does not mean that the *values* which the systems were in some ways trying to spread across the world—for example, democracy or human rights—depend on there being such systems. These values are something that we should cultivate, defend, and articulate ourselves, as Convoco has done in the last two years by discussing the ideas of equality and freedom, for example.[3] We shouldn't think therefore that the threat to the global or liberal world order is a threat to the values that it's trying to promote. And those values could remain even if the concept of "the West" starts to lose its point and its applicability.

My third point is about the climate crisis, and here we have reason to be very pessimistic. What we've learnt about this crisis is how hard it will be to make any real progress without any kind of international agreement. But this is a problem independent of anything that happens in relation to the decline of the above-mentioned institutions or systems. The sad truth is that the systems are largely impotent in making changes here.

The final point I want to make is that we will not make any progress unless we can maintain the distinction between fact and fiction, between truth and falsehood, and between what's real and what's not real. People may have their own opinions, but people may not have their own facts, their own reality. Of course, it's very difficult sometimes to find out what the difference is between truth and falsehood, between the real and the non-real. But that is part of what science, and knowledge-seeking more generally, are about. The fact that this is difficult to do should not make us reject or question the distinction between truth and falsehood. None of the crises we are faced with can be dealt with unless we keep in our minds a clear and absolutely unbending sense of the difference between the true and the false.

Notes

1 See Jörn Leonhard at the panel discussion "Which systems and institutions shape the world, and how appropriate are they for our times?" at the Convoco Forum on July 29, 2023 in Salzburg.
2 Corinne Michaela Flick, Introduction, in the present volume.
3 See Corinne Michaela Flick (ed.), *How much Freedom must we Forgo to be Free?* (Munich: Convoco! Editions, 2022); Corinne Michaela Flick (ed.), *Equality in an Unequal World* (Munich: Convoco! Editions, 2023).

CHAPTER 5

DEMOCRACY AT RISK, THE LAW AT RISK

STEFAN KORIOTH

I.

Democracies today have an obvious problem. Confidence that they and their institutions are capable of developing and implementing solutions to the wide variety of transformation-related problems in 21st-century societies is dwindling. If more democracies in the world are currently sliding into authoritarian forms of government than new democracies are emerging, this is an alarming finding. The return of war, fear of losing control in the face of invisible digital powers, fear of decline, the widespread suspicion that the real power does not lie with parliaments and governments but secretly in the hands of small influential groups and can no longer be democratically controlled—in light of these and other assumptions and changes, many citizens find the negotiation and decision-making processes of democracy outdated, ossified, impotent, and incompetent.

But is this really the case? In fact, democracy is the only framework of decision-making processes that offers the opportunity of solving problems when faced with inevitable change. What's more, democracy is the transformational form of government, because it is this very form that is able to recognize the dangers it faces, combat them, and overcome them. Crucial to this form is a specific, albeit fragile, combination of stability and openness, of deliberation and decision-making, of democratic forms and law in the constitutional state. If this combination is achieved, the "unassailable normative superiority"[1] of democracy over other forms of government organization becomes a reality.

II.

Today's constitutional state combines democracy with the rule of law. These basic principles mean various different things. Nevertheless, they are interrelated and interdependent. They must be realized jointly, even if tension or indeed conflict may arise between them. Dangers to democracy are dangers to the law and the rule of law. If the law is weakened, democracy is challenged.

Democracy is a flexible, dynamic principle by which a society organizes itself. It deals with decisions concerning the future that are developed through argument and counterargument, can be criticized and changed, have short- or long-term effects, and comprise more or less important choices. It is guided by the principle of majority rule. Decisions made democratically bring a society together and contribute to its self-determined identity. By contrast, the rule of law, with the basic requirement that all state power is subject to the law, is a stabilizing and persevering principle. The law provides forms, institutions, and procedures for the development and realization of democratic decision-making. Statute law is the main instrument of the constitutional state. The executive, the judiciary, and citizens are subject to its specification, which is binding until it is changed. This gives democracy shape, and predictable, specified paths to development. At the same time the law creates boundaries for democracy, especially in the shape of the constitution, which contains the fundamental specifications of a society, and primarily in the fundamental rights that statute law must satisfy. Fundamental rights cannot be removed by ordinary majorities. Thus the law shapes democracy and limits its power. At the same time, however, the law is also a product of democratic decisions, the result of the constitutive power of the people—in the rare case of the enactment of a new constitution and in the case of statute law the expression of the general political will.

These interdependencies characterize the constitutional state. Democracy without law can mean arbitrariness and the tyranny of the majority; but even a well-intentioned democracy would lack the means of control and organization without the law. The rule of law without democracy would be inflexible. The constitutional state provides the form democracy needs to be able to develop legitimacy for the law itself through its procedures. The law is an instrument of power, but it also normalizes power and even its own creation. This entanglement of democracy and the rule of law has a common premise and a common goal.

This concerns the freedom and equality of citizens, the ability to balance different interests with the same legal status as carefully as possible. But precisely because of this a society that is as free and equal as possible can be weakened not only by attacks on democracy and the law. Challenges to the inextricable link between the rule of law and democracy are particularly dangerous.

III.

Democracy is the form of government and society that is characterized by instability and inherent crisis. Apart from an unshakable foundation of values, everything can be challenged. There is a constant requirement to search for better solutions and rules as to how a society can coexist. Recognizing and naming critical developments are not dangerous, but necessary. In an authoritarian form of government things are different. The government must constantly give and enforce the impression that everything is going well and that tomorrow things can only get better, not worse. Any doubts about this must be suppressed if they cannot be channeled into an irrelevant issue. This requires money and instruments of power—police and violence if necessary. It can create its own problems, but apart from that it is not particularly demanding. In a democratic system, by contrast, everything is complicated, right down to the possibility of having a parallel debate that criticizes the way in which criticism of the existing situation is taken on board, discussed, or rejected. This is why descriptions of democracy never fail to point out that this form of government is difficult and permanently at risk.

From this perspective it is easy to see where the main danger to democracy lies today—in beliefs held by some in individual social groups who claim that their beliefs are universal and cannot be challenged. A typical tactic is to contrast a supposedly "true" democracy—of any kind—with the supposedly "formal" one of pluralism with its fluctuating definition of what is universally applicable. This goes hand in hand with declarations of inadmissibility and the proscription of other views, a reduction in spaces for reflection, the disparagement of science that provides advice and suggestions for solving problems, and the claims of "fake news." It also includes the justification of violations of "formal" law in the name of a higher "truth" or imperative. When, citing the supposedly established and correct will of the people, the cry goes up: "We are the people, who are you?" (as the Turkish president said during the election campaign), the democratic framework is broken. The same applies, albeit in the cause of a hardly controversial aim, when roads are blocked in order to draw attention to climate change and demand rapid responses. How we should face up to the consequences of climate change, like all other questions whether large or small, is subject to democratic deliberation. It must be accepted that this may involve delays and suboptimal solutions and that the immediate implementation of radical measures is impossible. If representatives of the activist group "Last Generation" are currently demanding immediate measures in opposition to even the majority of citizens and justifying violations of the law, they are invoking the conflict between a "substantive majority" and a (mere) "political majority". But this is exactly what destroys the context of discussion and decision-making in a democracy.

A somewhat less serious way of damaging democratic forms and institutions lies in the attempt to reduce the momentum of democracy outside of the obligations of the law. Anyone who invokes the silent majority or claims that there is no alternative to a particular decision is, precisely in this regard, also undermining the basic principles of free decision-making.

Social media, unlike the traditional mass media, tends to promote the absolute supremacy of partial interests, thereby narrowing the democratic space for reflection. Social media operates not with reflection and mediation, but rather immediacy, through an individualization that does not stop at separation, but considers itself to be advancing the general view. This "ideology of immediacy" includes the belief in the absolute correctness of one's own view of the world—the public sphere as a forum of differences falls apart, and this leads to a "derailed version of enlightenment."[2]

> Echo chambers, filter bubbles, alternative facts, fake news, deep fakes, political astroturfing, troll factories, conspiracy theories, hate speech and shit storms are keywords in a development in political communication that, in combination with US President Trump's political lie about the illegitimacy of democratic elections, led to the attack on the Capitol on January 6, 2021, and thus on parliament as the central institution of democracy [...].[3]

For two decades, Anglo-American authors in particular have been drawing attention to another kind of danger to democracy, one that comes from within democratic institutions. Colin Crouch claims that for a long time we have been living in a "post-democracy" in which the old institutions are just a facade to conceal interest-driven decisions taken by influential minorities:

> The idea of post-democracy helps us describe situations when boredom, frustration and disillusion have settled in after a democratic moment, when powerful minority interests have become far more active than the mass of ordinary people in making the political system work for them, where political elites have learned to manage and manipulate popular demands, where people have to be persuaded to vote by top-down publicity campaigns.[4]

David Runciman offers a pessimistic analysis in his book *How Democracy Ends*.[5] Some of this may be alarmist. However, it cannot be overlooked that a growing section of the population thinks that it has no influence over political decisions and that there is a growing contradiction between long-term tasks and short-term partial solutions. One dramatic example is the increasingly problematic future viability and sustainability of social security systems in Western constitutional states (and not just there) in light of changes in demography. In Germany, it has been known since the 1980s that old-age provision financed by pay-as-you-go contributions through a statutory pension can only work if there are enough contributors and if the burdens on them and on contributing employers remain tolerable. Equally, since the 1980s policy-making has been refusing to strike a new and necessary balance between generational equity and financial viability, with already drastic consequences. In 2022 the deficit in Germany's statutory pension insurance reached around 120 billion Euros. This had to be balanced out of the federal budget, that is out of tax revenue, consuming a quarter of the federal budget. If the existing rules do not change, the annual deficit will rise to between 180 and 200 billion Euros by the end of the 2020s. There are various suggestions for resolving the dilemma, which have advantages and disadvantages. They need to be discussed, but that is not happening. Of course, every democracy finds it hard to deal with long-term issues—it lives in the present, perhaps only until the next elections; it is supposed to produce modifiable decisions that will not prejudice future generations. However, refusing to make decisions about a long-term problem not only negates the deliberative qualities of a democracy. Sooner or later it necessarily also undermines trust in the problem-solving capacity of a democracy that is both free and committed to social equity. And when it comes to long-term issues that require sustainable solutions, non-decisions narrow the scope of action of future generations.

IV.

Dangers to the law are more subtle and not always easy to detect. A basic requirement of law that is anchored in and provides a framework for democracy is that legality and legitimacy coincide. What is applicable—legality—presumes objective appropriateness, perhaps even having truth and justice—legitimacy—on its side.

To this end, the applicable law must meet at least three basic requirements. First, it must be consistent, applicable without major difficulties, and crafted with reasonable care. It is apparently becoming increasingly difficult to live up to these secondary virtues of the law. The result is a decrease in the law's ability to exert control. The blame for this development lies not only with the legislators, but also with those subject to the law, who expect their respective situations and interests to be taken on board down to the smallest detail.

Second, the generality of rights, of the law in particular, must not be lost. Generality means that the law refrains from ruling on individual cases, the handling of which is a matter for those who apply the law. But generality also means equality of enforcement, especially in matters to which members of society are subject. Generality and equality are elementary manifestations of the law. People's belief in the legitimacy of the legal system diminishes when the law gains the reputation of promoting separation in society.

The third basic requirement of the law is one that is special and little-heeded. It is nevertheless of great importance. The interdependence of law and democracy means that the legal system requires two tiers of law. The first, overarching tier is the constitution, in which, in the section on fundamental rights, we find rights to freedom and equality that a society agrees to recognize; the state organization law establishes the procedures and institutions within which the democratic process can develop. The constitution should forego detailed regulations in favor of general frameworks. The constitution should be as constant as possible; amendments require qualified majorities. Below the constitution there is the second tier, the law as a policy-making instrument that can be changed quickly and that pursues specific objectives within the framework of the constitution. It is increasingly noticeable that the division of labor between the constitutional framework and specific statute law is disappearing. The constitution is losing its character as a predetermined framework for policy-making. Instead, policy decisions are being incorporated directly into the constitution in the form of verbose, detailed provisions in order to prevent such decisions from being amended by the legislature. This jeopardizes the character of the constitution as a framework and narrows the scope for movement in policy. Such shifts in the tiers of law can be found in the relationship between EU primary and secondary law, as well as in German national law. Since the beginning of the 1990s, the Basic Law has had to endure political compromises on specific questions being enshrined within it—questions that actually belong in ordinary statute law. Such undesirable developments are not easy to remedy; it is too tempting for politicians to incorporate hard-won compromises on controversial issues into the constitution, compromises that can then only be changed with the consent of all those involved. To the extent that this also reflects distrust in the effectiveness of political decision-making, the only riposte is that we simply have to "dare more democracy." The creative scope of legislators making ordinary statute law must not simply be capped by the upper tier of law.

V.

A liberal constitutional system is a "risky system."[6] It lives with solutions that can be revised in terms of time and content, with unreasonable demands and promises, with second-best answers, compromises, and with tentative attempts to improve the state of a society. This riskiness can be reduced, but never completely eliminated. Whether the institutions are sustainable is still an open question. *The Federalist Papers*, the summary of 18th-century political philosophy before the adoption of the US Constitution in 1788, described it as crucial whether "societies of men are really capable or not of establishing good government from reflection and choice, or whether they are forever destined to depend for their political constitutions on accident and force."[7] Whatever the case, a free society must be committed to ordered freedom. It is a dangerous illusion that an immediate path to the right solution might exist—whether by relying on the "real" will of a society or, as is currently the case, on a "substantive majority" that might cast aside the political majority. Two hundred years ago, against the backdrop of the terror of virtue of the French Revolution in 1793 and 1794, Hegel described this typical threat to ordered freedom and the consequences of such threats. Absolute freedom, he wrote, means that nothing lasts, not even objectives can succeed because every political form is questionable. The "sole work" of absolute freedom, Hegel continues, is the political death of a society, "a death too which has no inner significance or filling; for what is negated is the empty point of the absolutely free self. It is thus the coldest and meanest of all deaths [...]." What remains is "terror."[8] This has a universally applicable quality that should tell us to stay away from any dangerous promises of absolute rather than ordered freedom, of "substantive" rather than political majority.

Notes

1. Ulrich K. Preuß, "Die Bedeutung kognitiver und moralischer Lernfähigkeit für die Demokratie," in *Demokratisierung der Demokratie*, ed. Claus Offe (Frankfurt/M.: Campus Verlag, 2003), pp. 259 ff.

2. Torben Lütjen, "Populismus oder die entgleiste Aufklärung," *FAZ*, January 7, 2019, p. 6.

3. Jens Kersten, "Unbehagliche Betrachtungen von Staat und Verfassung," in *Theorie der Verfassungsgeschichte*, eds. Ino Augsberg and Michael W. Müller (Tübingen: Mohr Siebeck, 2023), pp. 89 ff., 101.

4. Colin Crouch, *Post-Democracy* (Cambridge: Polity, 2004), pp. 19–20.

5. David Runciman, *How Democracy Ends* (London: Profile, 2018).

6. Horst Dreier, "Der freiheitliche Verfassungsstaat als riskante Ordnung," *Rechtswissenschaft. Zeitschrift für rechtswissenschaftliche Forschung* 1 (2010), pp. 11–38.

7. Alexander Hamilton, James Madison, and John Jay, *The Federalist Papers*, no. 1, General Introduction (1787/88).
8. G.W.F. Hegel, *Phenomenology of Spirit*, trans. A.V. Miller (Oxford: OUP, 1977), pp. 360, 362.

CHAPTER 6

THE NEUROBIOLOGY OF TRUST

MARTIN KORTE

It is, needless to say, an unfortunate habit of some neuroscientists to think that, just because they are dealing with the most complex of all organs, they can give advice to other disciplines—let alone such venerable disciplines as economics or law. But it is also a good starting point for consideration, not as an end point of all actions and not in a normative way, to make suggestions as to how, at a time when many people mistrust economic, social, and political systems, we might design trust-building measures that draw on findings in psychological and cognitive science. What follows is an attempt at a practical guide—if we are allowed such a tongue-in-cheek formulation—on how to rebuild trust in our systems.

Trust is essential in every social interaction, whether private, at work, or with regard to economic transactions. Every day we are faced with decisions that require us to accurately assess another person's trustworthiness and with the challenge of simulating the real-world consequences of other people's actions within our brains. To do this we possess an area in the cerebral cortex, slightly hidden and folded back at eyebrow level, called the orbitofrontal cortex, which is responsible for assessing and regulating our own feelings and also acts as a mirror and simulation sensor for the thoughts and feelings of other people. Most importantly, this inwardly folded part of the prefrontal cortex checks whether someone we are interacting with is authentic. If this is the case, trust in a person's statements increases, but if the facial expression, physical posture, or intonation do not match what is being said, we lose this trust. A person's own belief in what they are saying is more convincing than any Powerpoint presentation.

Not only are our brains constantly calculating whether other people are being honest or are speaking with conviction, but our neural networks are also constantly making assumptions about what will be said and done next, or what is going to happen in the world in general. We see and experience what we expect to happen particularly quickly and with ease. This can lead to significant distortions in perception, especially since most of these internal filters (biases) inside our head operate unconsciously.

DISRUPTIVE TIMES REINFORCE COGNITIVE DISTORTIONS IN THE BRAIN

In a global market of increasing heterogeneity in terms of nationality, ethnicity, and numerous other social categories, it is extremely valuable to understand how implicit attitudes towards politicians, scientists, managers, or the boardrooms of major banks can promote or undermine society's trust in them, thereby implicitly influencing the decisions we make, that is either creating or abandoning trust in these systems.

Unconscious bias may sound like one of those ambiguous, difficult-to-understand scientific terms whose unwieldiness can make us not want to think about it—indeed this "not wanting to think about it" is actually inherent in the concept itself. Because if we open our eyes to what the brain is hiding from us, we can see how our unconscious biases influence almost every area of thought. These biases are the shortcuts our brains take to reach clear-cut conclusions quickly. For example, if we see a completely empty subway car, our brain may assume that it is empty for a reason and send us to the next car without further ado. In general, these mental leaps are essential because we cannot analyze every single sensory stimulus that our brain receives and then make decisions based on these analyses. However, there is also a dark side to this process: certain cultural prejudgments, or a bias against people with whom we have little direct contact, can become lodged in our brains without us realizing it, leading us to draw conclusions that might be inaccurate, incomplete, or even harmful, especially in times when we are seeing significant flows of migration.

In addition there are also distortions when it comes to the question of which experts we trust: for example, current research shows that when working in groups, we sometimes do not focus on a person's actual expertise, but on what we associate with expertise.[1] This means that, in our analysis of whether a person is an expert, characteristics such as confidence, extroversion, or how much someone speaks can outweigh proven knowledge. Conversely, sometimes we don't trust people simply because they tend to express their theories in an introverted manner along with their own uncertainties.

In other words, our brains can instinctively trust people just because they sound like they know what they're talking about. An experiment has shown that "airtime"—the length of time someone spends talking—is a stronger predictor of perceived influence than actual expertise.[2] In other words, who we trust doesn't just reflect how trustworthy and knowledgeable someone is, but also who we are and what unconscious biases we have.[3]

As with many of our behaviors, whose reflexive automatism is hidden from us by the brain, recognizing that we are susceptible to mental traps is the first step to overcoming them. For example, we can train ourselves to look out for signs of why we trust some people (who may also be the representative of a certain industry sector or social/cultural group) and not others. The most important thing is that we have to learn to catch ourselves (and others) when we are taking mental shortcuts. We need to take a step back mentally when following people who only appear authoritative (either because they radiate confidence or dominate the conversation) and ask ourselves whether they are truly trustworthy. Can they provide references to back up their claims? Are they talking around certain issues rather than addressing them directly? In short, if we catch ourselves being drawn to the arguments of someone who is extrovert and loud, we should question our trust in these arguments without ruling out the possibility that even someone who talks loudly may be right.

TRUST UNDER STRESS

The individual stress level of a person, organization, or society also influences trust and the creation of it. Few physiological conditions are as much of a double-edged sword as the stress response orchestrated by the brain. With the onset of a stressful event, a wide range of adaptations are mobilized throughout the body. Much of this is due to the activation of the sympathetic nervous system that secretes adrenaline and noradrenaline, as well as the release of glucocorticoids, such as the familiar cortisol, by the adrenal glands. If the event is an acute physical crisis (for example, sprinting to escape a predator or after a meal), the stress response is absolutely crucial to survival. But when the same stress response is activated chronically, the result is an increased risk of cardiovascular, gastrointestinal, immunological, and reproductive disorders. This dichotomy between the positive short-term effects of the stress response and its harmful chronic effects also extends to the brain. Research originally focused on the hippocampus, where an acute stress response improves the supply of oxygen and glucose and facilitates memory formation. By contrast, chronic activation of the stress response (mainly through the effect of glucocorticoids) impairs memory and causes atrophy of hippocampal neurons, which massively reduces the computational capacity of memory processes from storage to retrieval.[4] This means that the individual is less able to both recall and store knowledge, which means they are less capable of learning. Especially in times of massive upheaval, such as we are currently experiencing, the resulting chronic stress reduces human storage and memory functions.

Another type of dichotomy between short-term effects and chronic effects occurs in the amygdala, which centralizes the acute stress response for both body and brain. The chronic stress response leads to the structural growth of amygdala neurons, thus increasing the risk of anxiety disorders of the cerebral cortex: working memory is disrupted, judgment is impaired, and coping strategies are limited to habits, routines, and reflexes, i.e. people stick to stereotypical solutions to problems, even if these prove to be ineffective.[5] This latter effect involves inadequate cost-benefit analysis which creates a bias towards risk-taking, and is particularly pronounced when high levels of stress take control of actions, increasing the likelihood of impulsive, unreflective behavior, and perhaps explaining why in times of lack of trust in social systems and in times of uncertainty aggressiveness within a society increases. These shifts can also be convincingly shown in experiments on animals, in which intense stress or increased glucocorticoid load in laboratory rats is maintained for weeks or longer. In certain circumstances, the amygdala and frontal lobe may undergo permanent structural changes. Under chronic stress, new synaptic contacts grow in the amygdala, increasing its influence, while the frontal lobe loses synaptic contacts and thus loses control over the amygdala.[6]

In addition to the impacts on individual health, society too is affected. Chronic stress makes both people and animals less pro-social. For example, mice show a reduction in their pain threshold when they are near another mouse that is also experiencing pain. However, this pain resonance only occurs when the other mouse is familiar (i.e., a "cage mate"), as opposed to an unfamiliar mouse.[7] In other words, the social stress caused by an unfamiliar mouse limits the ability for "empathy-like" behavior. This same phenomenon was also observed in people: if the glucocorticoid level increases due to stress, empathy decreases and people feel less compassion for others.[8] Stress therefore limits consideration for others; for example, when subjects are exposed to an experimental social stressor, it causes them to make more self-centered decisions.

So chronic stress makes humans and mice more anxious, aggressive, selfish, and less empathetic. In addition, our ability to think self-reflectively and to assess risks correctly decreases. In a world struggling with the violent consequences of poor judgment and lack of impulse control, it is tempting to imagine that a better world might be possible through neurobiological interventions that block the stress response. But this is not possible from the point of view of everyday health. The stress response is vital when a person is faced with a severe physical challenge. The stress reaction can have a stimulating effect that promotes wakefulness and—if it occurs briefly—can heighten the senses. So it depends on whether we learn to deal with stress, whether we continue to see ourselves as agents who act and not just react (autonomy reduces the stress reaction), and on whether we also continually seek phases of genuine calm in order to interrupt chronic stress through conscious breaks.

The detrimental effects of stress on decision-making are only a concern if we are not aware of them. It also depends on our evaluation of the stressors. Changes in living conditions can also be perceived as a challenge; new things can arouse curiosity. Threats cannot be ignored, but one can, indeed must, seek out breaks even in times of crisis, and it helps to have political leaders who give the impression that they are making decisions that promote security.

MENTAL ABILITY AND IQ IN UNCERTAIN TIMES

Why are more and more people decreasingly able to understand complex and diverse social challenges? One reason for this may lie in the depletion of our cognitive resources in uncertain times, a concept known as *scarcity*.

Scarcity describes situations in which we are psychologically stressed, which limits our ability to fully think through problems in their complexity as well as to think through the planning steps that are important for the future. This may happen, for example, when our economic resources are threatened, when we are distracted by feelings of hunger due to an overly restrictive diet, and also when there are conflicts in relationships.[9] Unfulfilled needs can also capture our attention to the point of impairing our ability to concentrate fully. In such situations, the ability to think through alternative courses of action is limited, as in the example of a chess player who, when dealing with personal problems, can plan only six moves ahead rather than twelve.

Internal distractions resulting from scarcity can arise in particular during periods of uncertainty and major upheaval, as has been the case consistently over the past three years. Scarcity in one area of life means that we have "less intellect" available to apply to other aspects of life. This uncertainty can affect trust in systems or other people. The impact of scarcity can also be understood as a reduction in "mental bandwidth." Our cognitive bandwidth refers to our capacity and ability to think through decisions, stick to plans, and resist temptations, and is therefore closely linked to willpower. It correlates with performance in intelligence tests, as well as with impulse control—uncertain times also make social interaction more aggressive. Scarcity is caused by a powerful goal, namely to limit all other mental "construction sites" when dealing with urgent dangers that, perceived atavistically by the brain, are life-threatening.

Uncertain times bring threats to status or autonomy that limit the bandwidth of both the human ability to think and to show empathy.[10] Of course, such complex effects cannot be pinpointed to a single area of the brain, but the decrease in neuronal activity in the orbitofrontal cortex and an increase in activity in the amygdala do seem to limit the bandwidth of human ability to analyze problems to a considerable extent. In evolutionary terms, it may make sense in life-threatening, stressful situations to consider only the immediate future and to be less compassionate, but unfortunately this is not particularly helpful when complex human cultures have to make the right decisions for the future and trust people who can make these decisions.

To illustrate these effects, I will describe a classic experiment that looked at how our willpower is compromised when we are internally distracted. Test subjects were given a memory task. One group of people was asked to remember a two-digit number, another group a seven-digit number. The subjects were then taken into a lobby area to await further testing. In front of them in the waiting area were cakes and fruit. The real test was which food they would choose while repeating the numbers in their head. The test subjects with the two-digit number chose the fruit in most cases. Those whose attention was focused on repeating the seven-digit number chose the cake 50 percent more frequently—incidentally, these were nutritional science students. When our mental bandwidth is being used for something else, as in this case for repeating numbers, we have less capacity to stop ourselves from making short-term but knowingly harmful decisions.

In another test battery, both low- and high-earning subjects were examined in terms of their intelligence and logical thinking skills. These tests showed that both groups performed roughly equally well on intelligence tests when they were asked to solve a relatively "innocuous" problem concerning money. However, there were strong differences among those who the researchers had confronted with larger financial losses: low-income earners mastered the mental tasks much more poorly than test subjects with better incomes.[11] Expressed as a rule of thumb, people who are worried about the future make plans with fewer courses of alternative actions.

Equally, business data from companies confirms how important trust is, in this case in the "company system." Compared to employees in companies with low trust, employees with high trust in the company report 74 percent less stress, 106 percent more energy at work, 50 percent higher productivity, 13 percent fewer sick days, 76 percent more commitment, 29 percent more life satisfaction, and 40 percent less burnout.[12]

This shows why it is so important to actively create trust when we find ourselves in threatened, disruptive, and changing worlds. Scarcity is the basis of many current problems; worries about the future and security, or simply fear of everything that we don't understand, come together as a problem for society as a whole. It affects many people at the same time and can therefore have a measurable effect on economic and political decisions.

It is therefore all the more important that politics in uncertain times does not just concentrate on reaching compromises on secondary issues. If we want to maintain trust in social systems, we have to focus on the problems that cannot be solved with minimal consensus. If the bandwidth of brain performance is smaller, the airtime must be used wisely, otherwise too many people will fixate only on their own situation and overlook the consequences of their actions for the greater whole. The cognitive bandwidth of thinking in terms of alternative courses of action has a significant impact on a range of potential behaviors, even those that would normally come under the heading of personality or talent, such as patience, tolerance, attentiveness, and dedication. The financially strapped student who answers a few simple questions on a test incorrectly looks incompetent or even lazy. But it could just as well be that such a person is under a lot of cognitive stress. The problem is often not just coming from a specific person but must also be seen in the context of cognitive scarcity.

Perhaps the more profound lesson is to focus on what's important and to promote just a few key messages that are well-founded and authentically delivered, reinforcing them through repetition.

Notes

1. Kalil Smith, "Why our Brains Fall for False Expertise, and How to Stop it," *Strategy+Business*, 5.3.2018, https://www.strategy-business.com/article/Why-Our-Brains-Fall-for-False-Expertise-and-How-to-Stop-It (accessed November 21, 2023).

2. Ibid.

3. Damian A. Stanley, Peter Sokol-Hessner, Mahzarin R. Banaji, and Elizabeth A. Phelps, "Implicit Race Attitudes Predict Trustworthiness Judgments and Economic Trust Decisions," *Proc Natl Acad Sci USA*, 108 (19), 2011, https://www.pnas.org/doi/10.1073/pnas.1014345108 (accessed November 21, 2023).

4. Eun Joo Kim and Jeansok J. Kim, "Neurocognitive Effects of Stress: a Metaparadigm Perspective," *Mol Psychiatry*, 28 (7), 2023, https://pubmed.ncbi.nlm.nih.gov/36759545/ (accessed November 21, 2023).

5. Robert M. Sapolsky, *Behave: The Bestselling Exploration of why Humans Behave as they Do* (New York: Vintage, 2018).

6. Ibid.

7. Loren J. Martin et al., "Reducing Social Stress elicits Emotional Contagion of Pain in Mouse and Human Strangers," *Curr Biol*, 25 (3) 2015, pp. 326–32.

8. Ibid.

9. Nilli Lavie, "Distracted and Confused? Selective Attention under Load", *Trends in Cognitive Sciences*, 9 (2), 2005, pp. 75–82; Sendhil Mullainathan and Eldar Shafir, *Scarcity: The True Cost of Not Having Enough* (London: Penguin, 2014); Anuj K. Shah, Sendhil Mullainathan, and Eldar Shafir, "Some Consequences of Having Too Little" *Science*, 338 (6107), 2012, pp. 682–85.

10. Ibid.

11. Anandi Mani, Sendhil Mullainathan, Eldar Shafir, and Jiaying Zhao, "Poverty Impedes Cognitive Function," *Science*, 341 (6149), pp. 976–80.

12. Paul J. Zak, *Trust Factor: The Science of Creating High-Performance Companies* (New York: Amacom, 2018).

CHAPTER 7

WHAT ACCOUNTS FOR A DEMOCRATIC STATE'S ABILITY TO DEFEND ITS CORE VALUES?

BIRKE HÄCKER

Given the current widespread diagnosis of a "polycrisis" besetting our times, one experience stands out as particularly alarming and depressing. This is the realization that supposedly stable liberal democracies of the so-called "Global North" (formerly known as "the West") are nowhere near as stable as citizens living there have long assumed.

Metaphorically speaking, it has become clear over the past few years that the political layer of ice on which we have all been skating is extremely thin and fragile—much thinner and more fragile than most people could until recently have imagined. The basic societal consensus that underlies this political system has proven to be just as fragile. It is the ideal of a freedom-orientated system of liberal and social values focused on inalienable human rights, which on the one hand protects the will of each and every individual to determine their life according to their own preferences, and which on the other hand enables and supports individuals' active participation in social and political processes.

Not only has the expectation so far remained unfulfilled that these societal values and the concomitant political system would experience a more or less automatic worldwide spread in the wake of modern progresses in development and increased economic prosperity, thus self-evidently justifying their claim to universality over the course of time, they are, moreover, on occasion being severely tested even in those countries that regard themselves as the cradles of modern democracy and are keen to act as democratic "midwives" for others.

Against this backdrop, the question arises as to what actually accounts for the ability of a democratic state to defend its core values. For it is only when we keep this question in mind that we will be able to shore up the socio-political layer of ice that supports us and, where necessary, to protect it from being undermined, either externally or internally. The protective task is one for society as a whole if we want to preserve and foster the achievements of our liberal democratic system and to prepare it for the challenges that tomorrow may bring.

The present contribution aims to provide a brief outline of the background to the notion of a "defensive democracy," followed by some thoughts on the relevant "internal" and "external" stabilizing factors in the modern world.

THE NOTION OF A "DEFENSIVE DEMOCRACY"

The specifically German notion of a "defensive" or "militant" democracy can be traced back to the experience of the Weimar Republic. Its constitution is commonly said to have been so strongly committed to the principle of majority rule and political freedom that the Nazis in the National Socialist Party were able to undermine and infiltrate "the most democratic democracy in the world,"[1] thereby turning it into the exact opposite. As early as 1937, the constitutional lawyer and political scientist Karl Loewenstein, who had been removed from public service in 1933 and had then emigrated to the United States, coined the term "militant democracy." He linked it from the very outset with a special focus on fundamental rights (as well as, importantly, their limits!).[2] The mechanisms of the Weimar democracy, he suggested, had turned out to be a kind of "Trojan horse," enabling its enemies to take control of the *polis*.[3] Democracy itself, Loewenstein concluded, must be armed against such enemies.

After the end of World War II, the legal scholar Carlo Schmid put it similarly when speaking before the so-called Parliamentary Council, the constituent assembly drafting the West German constitution. He argued that a democracy must not provide opportunities and the conditions for its own abolition.[4] Accordingly, in order to ensure that democracy should "never again" be undermined, a whole series of safety mechanisms were incorporated into the Basic Law [*Grundgesetz*, abbreviated GG] of the Federal Republic of Germany, measures that were intended to consolidate, protect, and preserve the liberal democratic foundations of the newly constituted state. They include, among others, the so-called "eternity clause" in Art. 79 (3) GG,[5] the central constitutional position occupied by fundamental rights and the guarantee of their "essence,"[6] particularly the paramount importance of human dignity.[7] They further include the possibility of banning parties seeking to undermine the constitution,[8] the establishment of agencies specifically tasked with the protection of the constitutional order, the duty of loyalty to the state owed by civil servants[9] and, though only as a matter of last resort, "a right to resist any person seeking to abolish this constitutional order."[10]

This is not to conceal that the concept of a "defensive democracy" and the narrative underlying it has been variously criticized since the Basic Law came into force.[11] Nor should it just be taken as a given that the Weimar Republic actually failed because it afforded "too much" democracy, or indeed that the current Basic Law would have done better under comparable historical circumstances.[12] Challenging questions are being asked. Isn't the idea of a "defensive" or even "militant" democracy too repressive? Is the concept not perhaps primarily intended to keep out ideological opponents and to eliminate them? Is a given form of liberal government really entitled to preserve itself under all circumstances and by all means? Shouldn't it instead be based, first and foremost, on a broad social consensus?

Ernst-Wolfgang Böckenförde, one of Germany's foremost constitutional scholars of the post-war period, once stated in a different context that "[t]he liberal, secularized state depends on prerequisites which it cannot itself guarantee."[13] We may here take his dictum as an occasion to think about the notion of "defensive democracy" in a broader sense, one that is not specifically focused on Germany's Basic Law, but pertaining to liberal democracies more widely. What follows is an attempt to reflect on the factors that account for the resilience of modern democratic states committed to the rule of law (and, conversely, on factors that threaten these values). In doing so, a rough distinction will be drawn between factors providing "internal" stability, namely those that are embedded in the structure of the state or the constitution, and factors providing "external" stability, namely those that the state cannot guarantee, but which form part of its central foundations.

"INTERNAL" STABILIZING FACTORS

There is an answer to the critical challenge of whether it is really legitimate for a liberal democratic state to seal itself off hermetically from institutional changes to its core values and structure, and thus not to tolerate ideological opposition of a fundamental nature: any other approach would (or could potentially) amount to the state abandoning its own foundations, thereby assuming a very different character from the one it set out with. A constitution based on certain values and principles which are (pre-)posited as absolute and inviolable cannot of its own volition grant anyone the freedom actively to oppose these values and principles. If it did, it would no longer be the same constitution, because it would then make the very notion of inviolability inherently contingent on other factors, thereby questioning its own foundations.

This is, of course, not to deny a possibility that cannot logically be ruled out, namely that the said constitution—any constitution, in fact, regardless of its content—may at some point be overthrown and replaced by another constitution, a new constitution which does not share the same core values, and which is based on a set of completely different foundations. Yet such a transition from one constitution to another that is radically different will, on the above model, indeed be brought about by a "revolution" and by the power of facts; it cannot always be accounted for by smooth normative continuity. In this respect, the statement in Art. 146 of Germany's Basic Law ("This Basic Law [...] shall cease to apply on the day on which a constitution freely adopted by the German people takes effect") is no more than an attempt to salvage at least popular sovereignty, as the last vestige of the current constitution, and to secure its place at the heart of any future constitution.

As long as a democratic state operates within its own predefined structures and confines, it is at least not illegitimate, from a constitutional point of view, if it does whatever is necessary and possible to preserve and to strengthen these foundational principles and values from within. Its opponents have no normatively justified claim for the constitution to be "opened up," as it were, so as to allow for a seamless transition to a fundamentally different system of constitutional values and structures. Within the framework of Germany's Basic Law, it is therefore not merely legitimate, but perfectly consistent and indeed necessary, to demand from political actors a minimum level of loyalty to the constitution and, moreover, to combat forms of extremism with all available means. In addition to the longstanding, now all too familiar attacks on the constitutional order by the Far Left and Far Right, new forms of extremism have recently appeared, such as calls for the establishment of an Islamic state based on theocratic principles (so-called *Gottesstaat*),[14] posing new challenges for the agencies tasked with protecting the German constitution.

All this goes some way towards explaining why "defensive" constitutional states in particular, being unconditionally committed to *both* democratic values *and* human rights, (must) allow certain compromises in the wider field where different fundamental principles compete with each other. Though democratically elected and legitimized, the legislature may not and cannot touch or abolish the innermost core of fundamental rights and human dignity. Nor, on the other hand, may individual rights and freedoms be abused to undermine the foundations of the rule of law and democracy itself. One is the converse of the other.

How *exactly* the conflicting values are to be weighed up and balanced is, however, something that even the most "defensive" constitution does not specify in detail. Within the existing framework, there is significant leeway between the margins. It is rightly left to the interplay of political forces and institutions of the state to wrestle out the exact relationship and proper balance between conflicting postulates—for example that between democracy and freedom, or between freedom and equality, or that between freedom and security, particularly pertinent during the COVID-19 pandemic (all topics which featured in the last two Convoco! editions).[15] The very fact that this kind of political struggle takes place within a well-defined institutional, procedural, and substantive legal framework may itself be considered an important "internal" stabilizing factor.

This observation, in turn, suggests that the ability of a democratic state to defend its core values need not necessarily be down only to specific constitutional provisions, as envisaged by Karl Loewenstein and the fathers and mothers of Germany's Basic Law, but that it may well be a broader phenomenon. Isn't the mere fact of *having* a constitution itself a protective and stabilizing bulwark in a democratic state? Is it not perhaps a stabilizing factor that becomes stronger, the clearer and more widely understood the rules of a given constitution are? If that were the case, then it would be an argument for preferring a written constitution over an unwritten one.

Up until about a decade ago, such an argument would have met with almost unanimous opposition in the United Kingdom, the most prominent example of a modern Western democracy without a codified constitution.[16] The "constitution" of the United Kingdom consists essentially of two elements. On the one hand, a series of historically particularly significant parliamentary statutes relating to the organization of the state, so-called "constitutional statutes."[17] These are, however, technically no different from all other statutes of the realm and, importantly, do not take precedence over them. Nor are they specifically enshrined, so that they may simply be abrogated by the next parliament, provided only that this is done expressly rather than implied. On the other hand, there are a very large number of unwritten "constitutional conventions" in the United Kingdom, rules of good political behavior whose validity rests solely on the fact that they are universally respected and have over many generations been accepted without questioning. They are thus binding by tradition. In light of the United Kingdom's history and proud political heritage, which relatively early on combined the monarchical form of government with a remarkably strong parliament and a commitment to the rule of law, protagonists long believed that it was more important for the stability of a liberal democracy to have the relevant principles deeply rooted in popular consciousness and especially that of the political actors involved than to attempt to set out the core values and traditions in writing or even to enshrine them more firmly in some constitutional document.

Yet such beliefs are now crumbling. They have been shaken up by the experience of the last few years and in the eyes of many have actually turned into their exact opposite. The political earthquake unleashed by the Brexit referendum and the subsequent tussles over a new relationship with the European Union, some of which can only be described as completely chaotic, have made apparent the endogenous weakness of the unwritten British constitution. First of all, there were practically no guidelines and hardly any models to inform the "whether" and "how" of a national "advisory" referendum on continued membership of the EU.[18] Then, in order to suggest a stronger binding force than is possible in a system that traditionally revolves around the notion of "parliamentary supremacy" rather than popular sovereignty, interested political circles suddenly began invoking "the sovereignty of the people" over that of parliament and explained why the House of Commons had no political choice other than agreeing to a relatively "hard Brexit."[19] When a dispute arose as to whether the notification of the UK's intention to leave the Union in accordance with Article 50 of the Treaty on European Union (TEU) could be declared by government alone or whether it required the consent of parliament, this could not be settled without a decision by the UK Supreme Court (which ruled in favor of the latter).[20] Again, just a few years later, only a very stern Supreme Court judgment was able to prevent Prime Minister Johnson from unilaterally suspending parliament for over a month during a particularly critical phase of the exit process, citing the royal prerogative as allegedly justifying this obstruction to democratic mechanisms of government accountability and control.[21] Meanwhile, and partly as a result of the events just outlined, the independent judiciary is being openly attacked on a regular basis by members of the UK government and accused of interfering too much in the constitutional balance between the legislature and the executive powers of state. The problem is that no one really knows all the ins and outs of this balance, and it is unclear who is in the best position to pronounce on it.

Of course it must be said that, in a similarly exceptional political situation, any codified constitution might or would also have come under great pressure. However, the Brexit process demonstrates quite how wide the scope for interpretation is on the outskirts of mere unwritten "conventions," and how easily the constitutional system as a whole can become a potential target in the absence of a well-defined settlement on the division of state power. All of this suggests that the very existence of a constitutional document outlining the constitutional order in a systematic fashion and defining the interaction of the relevant powers should be seen as an "internal" stabilizing factor.

"EXTERNAL" STABILIZING FACTORS

In addition to stabilizing factors inherent in the constitution (whether in its content or its form), the ability of a democratic state to defend itself and its core values is undoubtedly also based in substantial parts on "external" factors. Although these are influenced by the constitutional setup, they cannot be wholly guaranteed by the state, as was mentioned above with reference to Böckenförde's dictum. Such "external" factors tend to be softer than the "internal." They are primarily rooted in a societal consensus and operate "bottom up" rather than "top down."

A central role in all this is played by the citizens and residents of a country because every functioning democracy depends on their participation. Their trust in democracy, the rule of law, and ultimately in the liberal state itself, and their willingness to support it, is the glue that holds the two layers—state and society—together. In the notional pact between citizens and state authorities, the two may appear to be on different sides, with individuals regularly exposed to state power; yet at the same time citizens should ideally see themselves as belonging to the state, forming an integral part of it, and sharing the core values that are also enshrined in the constitutional structure. Against this background, education in democratic responsibility, fostering an open exchange of opinions and respect for other members of society, is just as important as conveying an awareness of the "defensive positions" that individuals derive from their guaranteed fundamental rights and freedoms.

A country's media landscape, through which information and contributions to political discourse are both disseminated and "consumed," should on the one hand be sufficiently diverse and, on the other hand, maintain the necessary distance from the state and political parties, so as to reflect the full democratic spectrum of opinions. Then it, too, will have a stabilizing effect. History has shown time and again that direct state control of the media, potentially even its entire "synchronization" (*Gleichschaltung* as it was known during the Nazi era), is more than just a harbinger of authoritarian structures: it usually turns out to be symptomatic of an already pathological condition. With this in mind, we should all be concerned if and when newspapers, TV channels, or other news outlets lack critical distance or, more worryingly still, turn into a direct mouthpiece of certain individuals, parties, or interest groups.

Regarding media diversity, we also need to bear in mind that where information is primarily accessed via the internet, the risk of one-sided "exposure" is particularly high. This is because algorithms are used to work out what pieces and/or sources of information may be of particular interest to a given user, based on the individual's personal preferences as extrapolated from previous searches and other internet activity. As a result, people in their everyday lives are presented with different and very specific "packages" of media information, which—unlike in the past—are not consciously compiled by themselves (for example through choosing a particular newspaper or TV channel), but effectively by algorithms and third parties. Sooner or later, this almost inevitably leads people to start living in parallel universes and finding it hard to make out a common denominator with other members of their society. Particularly problematic in this context is the deliberate spread of misinformation (so-called "fake news"), because from inside a given "bubble" it tends to go unnoticed by an audience already predisposed towards it and thus to be absorbed largely without questioning.

To counteract such self-reinforcing and reality-distorting trends in an effective manner would be an important contribution to stabilizing a society's democratic discourse "from outwith." Regulation plays a role here; however, it is likely almost impossible to solve the problem through regulation alone. Instead, users themselves must be sensitized. They should be made aware of how to approach and deal appropriately with information channels, data filters, and personalization technology, and they should be encouraged to strive for real autonomy within the modern media landscape. That would help affected users to recognize self-reinforcing information loops and manipulation attempts, and it would prevent them being influenced heteronomously to an uncontrollable extent by information of doubtful origin.

It is true that the idea of self-determination is sometimes (mis)understood to mean that one must necessarily rebel against conventions and the establishment as such, and to be as non-conformist as possible. Yet what may well be part of the normal development of every teenager is a threat and "external" risk factor to democracy as well as the rule of law when it becomes a widespread permanent characteristic amongst the adult population. While once upon a time many citizens may have tried to be socially "well-adjusted" and to attract as little attention as possible, so much so that the German term *Spießbürger* (meaning conformist in a pejorative sense) was coined to describe them, the opposite trend appears to be gaining traction today.

A certain sensationalism and craving for attention—coupled with a social-media-fueled desire to express oneself and the above-mentioned phenomenon of "information bubbles"—has helped conspiracy theories of all stripes to become hugely popular. Growing groups of supposedly like-minded people enjoy casting themselves as non-conformists and are getting together to uncover alleged plots behind the settled beliefs, structures, and core values of "mainstream" society. Opinions that differ from their own and possible alternative explanations for a given issue or fact in question are then not used as occasions or reference points for a serious debate about realistic and indeed outlandish notions but are instead regarded as proof that the detected conspiracy is particularly effective.

Alongside conspiracy theories, we are also seeing a surge in other forms of resistance towards previously accepted facts and social values. For example, climate change and the COVID-19 pandemic are being still widely denied, and a disconcerting number of ordinary citizens in Western democracies appear suddenly to be developing a soft spot for dictators and autocrats (or perhaps now dare to openly admit it). The attempt to counteract this development with rational arguments often fails on account of a stubborn reluctance to take other viewpoints seriously or to engage with them in the first place.

Yet the ability and the will to understand what drives others, and to recognize that there is usually *something* to be said for a different opinion, is the cornerstone of every democracy. If the sociopolitical layer of ice that supports and stabilizes the democratic state "from outwith" is once again to become more robust, then it is by cultivating an open debate based on balanced, critically evaluated, and universally accessible sources of information. This culture of debate must include other points of view and accept even uncomfortable opinions, but it must also be one in which all relevant participants know and (can) trust that they are essentially pulling in the same direction, in the interests of everyone involved. This conviction, combined with the appropriate mutual respect, is the minimum requirement that needs to be met as an "external" stabilizing factor. Through it, the ability of a democracy to defend its core values is reinforced by society as a whole, allowing the political system to be sustained even in case of emergency.

Notes

1. Described as such by Dr. Eduard David (SPD), Minister for the Interior, at the plenary session of the Constitutional Assembly on the occasion of the adoption of the Weimar Constitution on July 31, 1919.

2. Karl Loewenstein, "Militant Democracy and Fundamental Rights" in *The American Political Science Review*, vol. 31 (1937) pp. 417 ff., 638 ff. Cf. also Karl Mannheim, *Diagnosis of Our Time* (London: Routledge & Kegan Paul, 1943).

3. Loewenstein, "Militant Democracy," p. 424: "Until very recently, democratic fundamentalism and legalistic blindness were unwilling to realize that the mechanism of democracy is the Trojan horse by which the enemy enters the city. To fascism in the guise of a legally recognized political party were accorded all the opportunities of democratic institutions."

4. This was why, according to Dr. Carlo Schmid, one should have "the courage to show intolerance towards those who want to use democracy in order to destroy it." Carlo Schmid, Speech to the German Parliamentary Council, September 8, 1948.

5. Art. 79 (3) GG [Basic Law]: "Amendments to this Basic Law affecting the division of the Federation into *Länder* [states within the Federation], their participation in principle in the legislative process, or the principles laid down in Articles 1 and 20 shall be inadmissible."

6. Art. 19 GG.

7. Art. 1 GG.

8. Art. 21 GG.

9. Art. 5 (3) and Art. 33 (5) GG in combination with the relevant provisions pertaining to the status and duties of civil servants.

10. Art. 20 (4) GG.

11. For a particularly critical approach, see Claus Leggewie and Horst Meier, *Republikschutz. Maßstäbe für die Verteidigung der Demokratie* (Hamburg: Reinbek, 1995). Contrast this with the more nuanced overview by Hans-Jürgen Papier and Wolfgang Durner, "Streitbare Demokratie" in *Archiv des öffentlichen Rechts*, vol. 128 (2003), pp. 340 ff., esp. pp. 362 ff.

12. See, for example, Udo Di Fabio, *Die Weimarer Verfassung: Aufbruch und Scheitern* (Munich: C.H. Beck, 2018), esp. pp. 6–7: "If the German Basic Law of 1949 had come into force in August 1919, it is doubtful whether the Republic would have even lasted until 1924 […]. If, on the other hand, the Basic Law had been in force from 1924 onwards, things would probably have been judged differently again; […] In the end, it will turn out that conventional assessments are by no means wrong, but often too simple or monocausal. The complex interplay between institutions and people, normativity and factuality, constraints and coincidences, deep national cultural currents and pressures of the moment do not admit for overly simple answers to the question of why the democratically constituted Republic collapsed." Cf. also the summary on p. 248: "The Weimar Republic suffered almost constant crises of considerable heft. Any constitutional order would have come under pressure and probably been distorted. In the foregoing analysis, the role played by the constitution in the failure of Weimar has proved smaller than the traditional narrative in the Federal Republic would have it."

13. Ernst-Wolfgang Böckenförde, "Die Entstehung des Staates als Vorgang der Säkularisation" in Ernst-Wolfgang Böckenförde, *Recht, Staat, Freiheit: Studien zur Rechtsphilosophie, Staatstheorie und Verfassungsgeschichte* (Frankfurt am Main: Suhrkamp, 1991), pp. 92 ff., 112.

14. See, for example, https://www.verfassungsschutz.de/DE/themen/islamismus-und-islamistischer-terrorismus/

islamismus-und-islamistischer-terrorismus_node.html and https://www.verfassungsschutz.niedersachsen.de/startseite/extremismus/islamismus/islamismus-151719.html (both accessed April 2, 2024).

15. Corinne Michaela Flick (ed.), *How Much Freedom Must We Forgo to be Free?* (Munich: Convoco! Editions, 2022); Corinne Michaela Flick (ed.), *Equality in an Unequal World* (Munich: Convoco! Editions, 2023).

16. Other well-known examples are Israel and New Zealand.

17. Particularly the *Bill of Rights Act* of 1688, the *Acts of Union* of 1707 and 1800, the *Parliament Acts* of 1911 and 1949, the *Human Rights Act* of 1998, and the *Scotland Act, Northern Ireland Act and Government of Wales Act* of 1998.

18. Following two previous referenda in 1975 and 2011, respectively, the Brexit referendum of 2016 was only the third to be held at a national level in the UK. Some (rather rudimentary) statutory provisions regarding the procedure are to be found in the *Political Parties, Elections and Referendums Act* of 2000.

19. For a general discussion on the way the concept of "sovereignty" was instrumentalized in the context of Brexit, see Adam Cygan, "Legislating for Brexit: 'The People' versus Parliament?" in *Global Policy*, vol. 13 (S2) (2002), pp. 47 ff.; Julia Rone, "Instrumentalising Sovereignty Claims in British Pro- and Anti-Brexit Mobilisations" in *The British Journal of Politics and International Relations*, vol. 25 (2023), pp. 444 ff.

20. *R (Miller) v Secretary of State for Exiting the European Union* [2017] UKSC 5, generally known as the "Miller I" decision.

21. *R (Miller) v The Prime Minister* [2019] UKSC 41, generally known as the "Miller II" decision.

CHAPTER 8

DEMOCRACY IN DANGER?

PETER M. HUBER

The state of democracy—our democracy—is on our minds. In their book, *How Democracies Die*, Harvard professors Steven Levitsky and Daniel Ziblatt are not alone in considering democracy to be in serious danger, citing Donald Trump as an example, drawing on the experiences of the 1930s, and noting the developments in Hungary, Turkey, and Venezuela—and one might also cite Poland, Israel, and even Britain.[1] Equally, in the volume *Die Zukunft der Demokratie*, edited by Friedrich Wilhelm Graf and Heinrich Meier, authors such as Sabino Cassese, Dan Diner, Horst Dreier, Herfried Münkler, and Peter Sloterdijk emphasize that the future of democracy is no longer beyond doubt, and that it is in need of criticism but also of voices in support.[2]

Whether democracy in Germany is actually in at this present time will be the subject of the following essay. In this, we should not be guided by alarmism. Of course, the axiom in communication science that "only bad news is good news" tends to lead us to invoke a crisis at least if we want to be heard. And indeed, we are surrounded by lots of crises: the climate crisis, the migration crisis, the demographic crisis, the crises of the Church, of political parties, of the social security systems, of the analogue economy, etc., etc. But does this also apply to democracy or, more precisely, to the constitutional state based on democracy and the rule of law?

Crisis, from the Greek κρίσις or κρίνειν, originally means a decision, a separation, or a differentiation in a particular situation. In any case, it requires a reliable diagnosis. With regard to democracy this requires that we first take a look at the pre-legal foundations of state authority (I). Based on this assessment, we can ask whether democracy and the rule of law in Germany are in crisis in the sense that their foundations are being eroded (II). In a third step, several dangers to these values and their reasons will be identified (III), before some suggestions for measures diminishing these dangers will be addressed (IV). The essay concludes with a look to the future (V).

I. PRE-LEGAL FOUNDATIONS OF DEMOCRACY

According to Ernst-Wolfgang Böckenförde's famous dictum, the liberal constitutional state lives by prerequisites which it cannot guarantee itself. This also applies to the democratic state as established by Germany's Basic Law [*Grundgesetz*, GG]. It depends on people's recognition as a legitimate authority and that its institutions are actually accepted in the sense of the *plébiscite de tous les jours* [daily plebiscite].[3] If this acceptance is eroded, the foundations of the constitutional state are also eroded and with it democracy is in danger.

I.1 LEGITIMACY AND ACCEPTANCE OF POLITICAL AUTHORITY

The legitimacy of any political system requires its recognition by society. It will only have a chance of lasting if—in the words of Georg Jellinek—it is supported by the willing obedience of those subject to authority. In this sense, every political order is based on the obedience of its subjects; "all its activity [...] is obedience transformed."[4] Authority can therefore neither be attributed to those subject to power alone nor to any ruler, even the most absolute dictator. It always owes its creation and existence to the interaction of both. As Jean Jacques Rousseau puts it: even the strongest is "never strong enough to be always the master unless he transforms strength into right and obedience into duty."[5] Against this background, authority finds its correlate in the obedience of those subject to power or, in a more modern perspective, in its acceptance by the citizens. Only authority that is perceived as justified and legitimate is accepted by those subject to it.

I.2 THE CONSTITUTION AS THE BASIS OF LEGITIMATE RULE

In this respect, the constitution can be an instrument for establishing legitimacy. As an act that creates order and a programmatic foundation and structure, aiming to give a society a legal basis in a concrete historical situation,[6] the constitution serves to establish and secure authority. It is based on a decision by the political forces that determine the process of drafting the constitution, groups that try to be permanently settled and at the same time must be controlled by this process. In this way, the constitution ensures the legality, effectiveness, and systematic exercise of authority.

However, the constitution also serves to connect the system of authority it establishes with the social norms and interests of individuals,[7] thereby guaranteeing its legitimacy. This presupposes that it succeeds in bringing and maintaining the constituted system of authority in accordance with the conditions and expectations of society.

I.3 RECOGNITION BY THOSE SUBJECT TO AUTHORITY

In a modern constitutional state, the people bear the "constituent power," the *pouvoir constituant*, as defined by Abbé Sieyès. A constitution is therefore only worthy of recognition because and to the extent that it can be attributed to the people and is actually perceived as such, and Max Weber's distinction between traditional, charismatic, and legal authority comes down to the third alternative. In a constitutional state based on democracy and the rule of law a belief in the validity of rationally created rules as the basis of the authority is indispensable. This form of government has a crisis-tested and resilient source of legitimacy that should not be underestimated. This adds to sociological and historical circumstances, such as a shared language and history, the idea of a nation and its self-determination, the pursuit of freedom and equality of all citizens made possible by this framework, and the belief that both the individual and the collective "pursuit of happiness" and justice can best be realized in this way.

On the other hand, however, legitimacy and acceptance of the constitutional state also depend on the fact that it can, at least in part, deal with a society's current challenges in terms of external and internal security, social welfare, and environmental protection. Even a democracy may become a "failed state" not worthy of recognition in the eyes of its citizens if it doesn't successfully cope with these challenges. As is well known, the *ancien régime* in France fell because of the price of bread, the Weimar Republic because of mass unemployment, and the GDR due to its apparent inability to meet the economic expectations of its citizens. Conversely, the so-called economic miracle in the "old" Federal Republic of Germany after 1950 helped to give legitimacy and recognition to the constitutional state shaped by the Basic Law.

II. CURRENT CONDITIONS
II.1 A STABLE SYSTEM FOR 75 YEARS

May 23, 2024, marks the 75th anniversary since the *Grundgesetz* came into effect. It has been in effect significantly longer than all other constitutions since the founding of the German nation state in 1867/71 and has also proven to be flexible enough to absorb the political, economic, and social changes since 1949. It has survived some epoch-making turning points, from rearmament in 1955 to the emergency laws of 1968, the abortion debate in the 1970s, reunification in 1990, the emergence of new parties, deployments of the Bundeswehr abroad, the terrorism of the Red Army Faction and Islamism, and the phasing-out of nuclear energy, which was fought over intensely for decades.

On the basis of the *Grundgesetz* it has been possible to turn the legal system, which largely dates back to imperial times before 1918, upside down and to make the individual its focus. Today, unlike before 1949, issues of public law are no longer primarily looked at from "above," from the perspective of the state, politics, and administration, but from "below," from the perspective of the citizens affected, their rights and interests. This paradigm shift has its roots in a modified understanding of the state that the Constitutional Convention of Herrenchiemsee in 1948 summed up as follows: "The state exists for the sake of the individual, not the individual for the sake of the state."

CONDITIONS FOR SUCCESS

The fact that Germany has been fortunate with its *Grundgesetz* over the past 75 years is certainly due to the fact that this statute contains a number of clever provisions for the stabilization of political institutions. But no matter how smart the constitution is, it is not enough to guarantee its success in society. It must also be accepted by society and its values must be lived.

The conditions for success undoubtedly have profited from the absence of existential challenges. The Federal Republic of Germany has been spared wars, coups, uprisings, and separatism. Therefore, the constitutional system was able to consolidate and could be developed step by step. Moreover, after two world wars and a dictatorship, German society was relatively homogeneous and social tensions were low, so that people's interests in the first decades were less divergent than today. The so-called economic miracle of the 1950s and 1960s and the associated "Rhenish model" of capitalism did the rest.

But it was also important that politicians took and still take the constitution seriously. Sixty-seven amendments of the Basic Law provide evidence that politicians respect the constitution which has proven to be a "living instrument" in the proper sense of the word.

ENFORCEABILITY AND FLEXIBILITY

Another reason for the success of the *Grundgesetz* is that it is directly applicable law. It must be applied by all constitutional bodies, authorities, and courts.[8] The fact that this has been so resoundingly successful is due not least to the Federal Constitutional Court [*Bundesverfassungsgericht*], which among others has been set up following the American model. With its very far-reaching competences, even by international standards, which subject every administrative act and every court decision to its control, the *Bundesverfassungsgericht* to a large extent has been responsible for the implementation of the above-mentioned constitutionalization, i.e. the re-interpretation of a legal system that largely pre-dates the constitution (for example, civil code [BGB], criminal code [StGB], code of civil procedure [ZPO], code of criminal procedure [StPO]). Today, almost every policy issue can be re-framed in terms of the constitution, from the merger of the states of Baden, Württemberg-Baden, and Württemberg-Hohenzollern to the *Land* of Baden-Württemberg via the dissolution of parliament, the deployment of the army abroad, statements by federal presidents and members of the government, to bans on political parties. The now 164 volumes of the official collection of decisions reflect the history of the Federal Republic of Germany.

CONSTITUTIONAL PATRIOTISM

The successful establishment of the democratic constitutional state after 1949 and its largely effective response to social challenges have led to a growing awareness since the 1970s and 1980s that the integrity of the Basic Law represents an inherent value that must be defended. Thus the *Grundgesetz* developed in society's consciousness from a transitional technocratic statute with little emotional heft into a valued, if not revered, permanent constitution, and something we might call "constitutional patriotism" has emerged. Like the US with its 226-year-old constitution of 1787, Germany with its now 75-year-old *Grundgesetz* proves that a "successful" constitution can become the basis and crystallization point of constitutional patriotism and civic pride.

II.2 CRISIS SYMPTOMS
NO INCLINATIONS TOWARDS AN "ILLIBERAL DEMOCRACY"

Germany currently neither suffers from a state crisis nor is the constitutional order in danger. She has (so far) been spared from a fundamental, populist challenge to the constitutional state, as we have had to witness in Hungary, Poland, Israel and earlier in Russia and Turkey. These states' rulers, having gained power through (more or less) democratic elections, have sought to extend their temporal power that is typical in a democracy by removing constitutional limits of majority rule. The German government, however, has made no attempt to weaken the *Bundesverfassungsgericht*, nor tell the judiciary to fall into line, nor hijack public broadcasting and other media. There has been no interference with universities or an erosion of civil liberties.

On the contrary, there is still a broad social consensus in favor of a liberal democracy contained by the rule of law. The denigration of liberal democracy as an obstacle to the implementation of the will of the majority and the plea for an "illiberal" democracy in which the supposed will of the majority—as identified by those in power—is the standard for all things (this links it to the US debate on the "counter-majoritarian difficulty" of the judiciary) has so far been met with little interest. There is widespread agreement that the democratic constitutional state is based on a dialectic between the will of the majority and the commitment to the rule of law. In such a form of government, political authority based on the will of the majority is only permissible if legally constituted and bound to the rule of law, the constitution being part of it. It therefore must not ignore the constitutional guarantees the rule of law entails, because only they—fundamental rights and legal protection—enable the kind of open democratic debate in which the minority of today can (once again) become the majority of tomorrow. In order to ensure that power is limited in time[9] and that the respective majority is in constant competition with the minority and always faces the possibility of becoming the minority itself, the majority must not close the door by which it has entered into the room where it gained its authority.

SOCIAL POLARIZATION AND DECLINING ACCEPTANCE

However, the success of the constitutional state since 1949 is no reason to rest on our laurels, because there certainly exist phenomena that cast shadows over the reassuring picture we have sketched so far.

Like other Western countries, Germany has been experiencing increasing social polarization for about a decade, which, if it continues, in the long run could also endanger the acceptance of the constitutional state.

This development first became noticeable with the Euro crisis after 2010; it was later fueled by the refugee crisis after 2015 and the COVID-19 crisis between 2019 and 2022. Dealing with the climate crisis is also an issue. In most of these constellations, the war in Ukraine being the only exception, we can see an increasing alienation between "woke" (leftish or Green) circles in the big cities such as Berlin and Hamburg, several university towns and their proponents in politics and the media, on the one hand, and the rest of the population who lives in small- and medium-sized towns and in the country, on the other.

Between those extremes, the ways, conditions, and perspectives of life have become increasingly divergent. On the one side there is a well-off, university-educated, cosmopolitan circle that thinks radically from the perspective of the individual and is skeptical about communities such as family, nation, or Church;[10] while on the other side there are still traditional structures of a petty-bourgeois and/or middle-class society in which people know, even beyond the agricultural setting, that they depend on each other and on healthy communities, structures, security, and predictability.

The gap between those "anywheres" and these "somewheres"[11] is continually growing and is capable of undermining the readiness to accept majority decisions by democratic institutions. At the same time the constitutional state and its institutions are losing support. Even the judiciary, including the *Bundesverfassungsgericht*, is perceived and discredited by populists as an instrument of those in power, as if they played a role comparable to that in totalitarian states such as Venezuela, Russia, or Turkey. Although this image depicts a grotesque distortion of reality, it is employed by representatives of the party *Alternative für Deutschland* [AfD – Alternative for Germany], but also by the more left-wing lecturers in constitutional law, especially with regard to the decisions the

Bundesverfassungsgericht has made in the context of COVID-19.

Other highly emotionally charged settings for this clash include the attempt to establish gender-appropriate language in the public sphere, the media, schools, and universities; the debates about the biological or social determination of gender;[12] dealing with militant Islam;[13] and many more. Public broadcasting is—not undeservedly—seen by large parts of the middle-class and right-wing populist spectrum as a propaganda tool for the current ruling majority. Shrill voices calling for it to undergo cutbacks or even its abolition are finding a correspondingly growing audience. Traditional instruments and forms of identity creation such as the flag or national anthem, etc., are denounced by the leftish and the Green spectrum as outdated, nationalist, and colonial and are handled even by state authorities so tentatively that large parts of society no longer dare engage with them because they do not want to be suspected of extremism. In addition, there exists an East/West antagonism in Germany which was previously fueled by the Socialist/Left Party [*PDS/Linke*] and today by the AfD.

III. CONSTITUTIONAL CAUSES?

The causes of unease among a growing part of society are many and varied. They mainly have to do with globalization and its consequences, with short-sighted policies that have not responded decisively enough to the specific challenges of globalization, but also to a certain extent with the actual way democracy works.

III.1 LACK OF RESPONSIVENESS IN THE POLITICAL SYSTEM

According to the principle of popular sovereignty laid down in Art. 20 para. 2 GG, all state authority in Germany is derived from the German people and is exercised by them through elections and votes as well as through special bodies of the legislature, the executive, and the judiciary. A right to democratic self-determination (Art. 38 para. 1 sentence 1 GG) guarantees individual citizens an effective say in affairs of state.[14]

Despite all the theoretical exultation of democracy in the jurisprudence of the *Bundesverfassungsgericht* and academia, the output dimension of this principle seems sobering: the fact that a migration crisis can be dragged out for almost a decade against the will of the overwhelming majority of the people (according to all opinion polls) does not suggest a particularly high level of responsiveness in the political system. There are other examples too: the ineptitude in combating the pandemic, the difficulties in procuring vaccines, climate protection policy, or the final phasing-out of nuclear energy at the height of the energy crisis. There might have been good reasons for all measures taken in these areas. However, it cannot be denied that citizens have primarily been spectators in all these areas and that they have developed a growing feeling of powerlessness.

LITTLE OPPORTUNITY FOR INFLUENCE

In fact, the democratic portfolio is rather modest: the Bundestag is elected every four years (Art. 39 para. 1 sentence 1 GG), the European Parliament and state parliaments every five, and local councils usually every six. The political establishment has pushed through an extension of the legislative periods everywhere at state level and is also attempting to do the same at federal level. As a result, the Bundestag's level of democratic legitimacy is declining—nothing politicians would really care about. Albeit permitted by the *Grundgesetz*, politicians (following Theodor Heuss's misinterpretation of the Weimar period) have also refused to introduce plebiscites and referenda in the Basic Law so far.[15] Instead they have installed instruments with a placebo effect that are intended to simulate democracy like citizens' councils [*Bürgerräte*] drawn by lot. What is left is that citizens can resort to the exercise of those fundamental rights that entail a political dimension: freedom of expression, information, broadcasting, and the press, or involvement in political parties.

Against this background it becomes clear that politicians have little "fear" of the electorate and that they can confront the latter safely with a supposed lack of alternatives. However, this is poisonous for the acceptance of democracy. Democracy requires alternatives!

PARTOCRATIC MODIFICATION OF THE INSTITUTIONAL STRUCTURE

In addition, the Basic Law has not only taken the reality of political parties seriously, recognizing them as institutions of constitutional life in Art. 21 GG. They are considered as intermediaries between the people and the organs of state and as indispensable in ensuring the accountability of the latter to the German people. After all, the constitutional regime of political parties has proven to be open enough to enable the permanent establishment of new political parties: the Greens in the 1980s, the Left Party in the 1990s and the AfD during the last ten years. But it has also brought about a partocratic modification of the institutional setting of the *Grundgesetz*, in which coalition agreements and rationales have become more important than the pragmatic implementation of the will of the majority according to the written rules of the constitution. This too comes at the cost of acceptance.

MARGINALIZATION OF INDIVIDUAL MEMBERS OF PARLIAMENT

The individual members of parliament—actually the linchpin of representative democracy—see themselves as marginalized in a very hierarchical system that is *de facto* determined by the government and/or parliamentary group leaders. Theoretically, according to Art. 38 para. 1 (2) GG, members of parliament are "representatives of the whole people, not bound by orders or instructions and responsible only to their conscience." In practice, as long as they do not hold other positions, the individual member is only one out of 736 members of parliament, in other words a *quantité négligeable*. A member of parliament fighting for re-election has to worry more about the goodwill of the party and parliamentary group leaders than about the approval of the electorate. It is therefore rational if they orientate themselves rather towards the will of their political "superiors" than towards the will of their constituency, given they represent one. This impacts negatively on the most important lever of citizens' political self-determination and promotes feelings of powerlessness among them.

III.2 HYPERTROPHY OF THE LEGAL SYSTEM

A different challenge that is increasingly paralyzing state institutions and thereby threatening the acceptance of democracy is the hypertrophy of the legal system. Of course this phenomenon is not new. Montesquieu is already credited with saying that if it is not necessary to make a law, it is necessary not to make the law. However, the scale of the problem has augmented fundamentally: about 150,000 poorly coordinated legal measures of the European Union, 15,000 provisions of federal law, and around 8,000 regulations of state law make it increasingly impossible for executive authorities and the judiciary, but above all for those subject to the law, to obey and implement applicable law reliably and within a reasonable period of time. They undermine the principle of legality and turn laws, regulations, and directives—the constitutional state's most important steering instruments—into random generators whose output is almost impossible to determine in advance. This has a negative impact on legal certainty and encourages decision-makers either to ignore legal requirements or to choose an attitude of attentism,[16] which is in turn problematic for the acceptance of the rule of law.

III.3 LACK OF CLEAR RESPONSIBILITIES IN A MULTI-LEVEL SYSTEM

The problem is further complicated by the complexity of the multi-level system of political authorities in Europe. Within this system there are considerable difficulties in coordinating and clearly assigning competences to the five levels of European Union, federal, state, district, and municipality. If everyone has a say in everything, ultimately no one is responsible. This may certainly be attractive for the politicians in charge as it makes accountability impossible. With regard to democracy, it's a disaster, because it sends citizens and their concerns off on a Kafkaesque journey.

III.4 MORALIZATION

Last but not least, there remains the increasing moralization of political disputes, the discrediting of dissenting opinions, and stigmatization. Instead of explaining to citizens that denying climate change is nonsense, that courting Vladimir Putin results in the abandonment of the Western way of life, or that Germany's exit from the European Union would threaten the country's economic and political stability, people indulge in morally charged discussions about "firewalls." By labeling political adversaries as "enemies"—an echo of the darkest Weimar times—real and supposed extremists are pushed into a corner. This encourages their further radicalization and condemns state institutions to inaction in those areas in which adversaries too may have legitimate concerns. As the example of Thuringia shows,[17] the application of democratic voting rules to the election of a prime minister or the vote on a proposal from an opposition group can—if declared morally unacceptable —(in part) be prevented and with them the solution of a problem.

The effect of this moralization is that some parties are trapped in a kind of "Babylonian captivity" by the political ideas of the other side. This means that there is practically no alternative in terms of power politics. But democracy cannot function without alternatives.

IV. SUGGESTIONS FOR THERAPY

Against this backdrop, there are some suggestions for "therapy":

1. Forgoing further reductions in the level of democratic legitimacy by extending legislative periods.

2. Strengthening the responsiveness of representative democracy by reducing the dominance of partocratic rationales in parliamentary, representative, and electoral law, and strengthening the role of the individual member of parliament vis-à-vis the parliamentary group leadership and government.

3. Instruments of direct democracy may help to alleviate the partocratic distortion of the institutional structure of the constitution, and the associated deficits in the system of representation can also be alleviated to some extent.[18] They are not an alternative to parliamentary representation, but at best a selective supplement.

4. Legislators at all levels must ensure greater consistency in the law they enact. They must recognize and take into account that their regulations are aimed at the same citizens and that the latter must not have to deal either with contradictory orders or with a disproportionate accumulation of burdens. The doctrine of constitutional law has achieved little so far. It is all the more important that politicians recognize the risk to which they expose the constitutional state with their unbridled mania for regulation and legislation.

5. In addition, the distribution of competences between the European Union, the federal government, and the states must be taken seriously and designed to be as free of overlap as possible. The tendency of the European Commission as well as the European Central Bank to develop

broad-based rights of intervention in the administrative processes of Member States contradicts the necessity of a clear assignment of competences.

6. Not least, politicians need a certain degree of courage and willingness to take risks. Understandable firewalls against populists must not lead to a situation in which social and political ideas supported by the majority of society are no longer politically enforceable. That does not necessarily mean coalitions or tolerance agreements, nor does it require surrender into a coalition with the other side.

7. Even minority governments, although condemned by political scientists for the last 75 years, are not necessarily a bad alternative from a democratic point of view. It goes without saying that they are not attractive to those in power because they are fraught with too many uncertainties. But this cannot be the decisive point. Not only have Scandinavian countries in particular had good experiences with minority governments, but the latter would also put a (temporary) end to the subordination of institutions to the rationales of political parties, coalition circles, etc. and shift decisions back to where they belong—to parliament.

They would also noticeably slow down the legislative machinery and counteract the hypertrophy of the legal system that endangers democracy.

V. OUTLOOK

German democracy is not yet in crisis. But it is, as other democracies, going through troubled times, and there are recognizable dangers. Ultimately, it is up to all of us to avoid democracy plunging into crisis in the first place. We are the people and we, each according to our abilities, bear responsibility for ensuring that the conditions on which the constitutional state and its acceptance depend are maintained. This means making use of our democratic rights of participation, taking on board other ideas—of those who oppose us—and at least considering them by viewing political opponents only as such and not as "enemies," and by not allowing ourselves to be dissuaded from what we believe to be correct either by officials or by the proponents of the *juste milieu*. And, last but not least, we should trust in our constitutionally guaranteed fundamental rights.

Notes

1. Steven Levitsky and Daniel Ziblatt, *How Democracies Die* (New York: Viking, 2018).

2. Friedrich Wilhelm Graf and Heinrich Meier (eds.), *Die Zukunft der Demokratie. Kritik und Plädoyer* (Munich: C.H. Beck, 2018).

3. Ernest Rénan, *Qu'est-ce qu'une nation?* (Paris, 1882).

4. Georg Jellinek, *Allgemeine Staatslehre*, 3rd. edn. (Berlin, 1914), p. 426.

5. Jean-Jacques Rousseau, *The Social Contract*, trans. Maurice Cranston (London: Penguin, 2004), p. 4.

6. Peter Badura, "Staatsphilosophie" in Felix Unger and Franz Kardinal König (eds.), *Und wir haben doch eine Zukunft: Mensch und Natur an der Schwelle zum 3. Jahrtausend* (Freiburg: Herder, 1990), p. 291.

7. Ibid.

8. Art. 1 para. 3 and Art. 20 para. 3 GG.

9. On this cf. German Constitutional Court Decision [BVerfGE] 141, 1 (21, Rn. 53) – treaty override.

10. Andreas Reckwitz, *Die Gesellschaft der Singularitäten. Zum Strukturwandel der Moderne* (Frankfurt am Main: Suhrkamp, 2017).

11. David Goodhart, *The Road to Somewhere: The Populist Revolt and the Future of Politics* (London: C. Hurst & Co, 2017).

12. Statement by the Humboldt University, Berlin on July 4, 2022: On the cancellation of the lecture *Geschlecht ist nicht (Ge)schlecht: Sex, Gender und warum es in der Biologie zwei Geschlechter gibt* in the Long Night of the Sciences, 2022.

13. Statement by the University of Jena on September 14, 2023: On the interview with the *Tagesschau* spokesperson, Constantin Schreiber, in *Die Zeit*.

14. Cf. German Constitutional Court Decision [BVerfGE] 89, 155 (187) [1993] – Maastricht; 123, 267 (340 f.) [2009] – Lisbon; 129, 124 (169, 177) [2011] – EFSF and Greek bailout; 132, 195 (238 Rn. 104) [2012] – eA ESM; 135, 317 (386, Rn. 125) [2014] – ESM; 142, 123 (190, Rn. 126) [2016] – OMT.

15. Art. 29, Art. 118, Art. 118A, and Art. 146 GG.

16. Peter M. Huber, "Rechtsstaat" in Herdegen/Masing/Poscher/Gärditz (eds.), *Handbuch des Verfassungsrechts* (Munich: C.H. Beck, 2021), para. 6, note 108.

17. In Thuringia, the CDU opposition party had put two propositions to the vote in the state parliament, with the support of the AfD group: reduction in real estate transfer tax and minimum distance rules for wind turbines.

18. Peter M. Huber, "Direkte Demokratie? Gefahren und Chancen für das repräsentative System" in Henk Botha, Nils Schaks, and Dominik Steiger (eds.), *Das Ende des repräsentativen Staates? Demokratie am Scheideweg* (Baden-Baden: Nomos, 2016), pp. 293, 305 ff.

CHAPTER 9

HAVE CAPITALIST ECONOMIC INSTITUTIONS FUNCTIONED DURING THE CRISIS?

MONIKA SCHNITZER

How well prepared are capitalist institutions for crises? And how well do they function in an acute crisis? In crises especially, the question is often asked whether decentralized, private-sector systems may be at a disadvantage compared to planned, centrally organized systems that rely on a strong state. The experiences of recent years have made it clear that the state plays a crucial role in crises, even in capitalist systems. The question is why and to what extent the state fulfills this role.

To find answers to these questions, it makes sense to look first at how a capitalist economy works ideally, and what role the state plays in it in regular times. This leads to the question of why the state is particularly challenged in times of crisis, even in systems organized by the private sector, and whether the state fulfills this role ideally or what might stand in the way of this. Finally, we will attempt to assess the crisis management during the most recent crises and draw conclusions about how state capacity can be increased.

THE ROLE OF COMPANIES, HOUSEHOLDS, AND THE STATE IN A CAPITALIST ECONOMY

The interaction of supply and demand between private companies and households in free markets ideally characterizes the capitalist economy. The role of the state is to ensure legal certainty and the enforcement of private contracts based on defined property rights. However, the interaction of supply and demand via the market mechanism only leads to efficient market outcomes if certain conditions are met. For example, the efficiency of market outcomes is jeopardized if there is no functioning competition between market participants. Inefficient market outcomes or even market failures can also occur if those active in the market have different levels of information. Inefficiencies also happen if the actions of private actors have positive or negative externalities concerning other market participants.

These causes of market inefficiencies justify the state taking on a regulatory and supportive role in a market economy. By setting the framework conditions, the state defines limits for market actors and intervenes in a regulatory manner to ensure fair market conditions through competition policy and to correct market failures using the appropriate instruments. For example, it provides public goods and services that private companies do not sufficiently provide due to their positive externalities, such as education or security. As the Coase Theorem describes,[1] it is not necessary for the state to intervene *per se*. Instead, those affected can themselves negotiate how, for example, externalities in the case of environmental pollution can be compensated for and avoided. Private negotiations can therefore achieve an efficient market outcome, provided that there are no transaction costs associated with private coordination. This ideal example of a world free of transaction costs never exists in reality. The more potentially affected people have to be taken into account, and the more the information is asymmetric, the harder it is to find purely private solutions to these market inefficiencies.

THE IDEAL ROLE OF THE STATE IN MANAGING AND PREVENTING CRISES

If the state plays a vital role in the functioning of a market economy in regular times, this is particularly true in the event of a crisis. Whether and how well a capitalist system can cope with a crisis depends crucially on how well the state fulfills its role in crisis prevention and management. In a crisis, the balance of the market is disturbed, and suppliers and buyers have to adjust their coordination quickly. In the case of natural disasters, there are usually a large number of those affected who are unable to adjust their coordination themselves in the event of a crisis or only at great expense and cannot procure the necessary relief items or relief measures via the market. It is difficult to take appropriate precautions in the event of a crisis if it is unclear who might be affected by such disasters and should, therefore, be included in the costs in advance. Unsurprisingly, incidents of freeloading usually happen in such cases because everyone is counting on others to contribute to preventing disaster. Even when a disaster strikes, the extent of the damage is often unknown to the other actors.

This is where the state comes into play. In a crisis, it assumes the function of coordinating between the actors. It organizes aid, provides information and resources, and bears some of the costs of the crisis at the expense of taxpayers. So, during a crisis, the state functions as an insurance provider and ensures that the costs are at least partly met by society and that burdens are distributed fairly. Unlike private actors, the state monitors the totality of externalities and costs associated with the crisis.

The state also performs essential functions in the run-up to a crisis, on the one hand, by avoiding crises, and on the other, by preparing for crises that cannot be completely avoided. Crisis avoidance includes, for example, setting appropriate framework conditions for improvements in climate protection and taking measures to avoid flood disasters. Preparing for crises includes, among other things, purchasing protective equipment in the event of a pandemic or ensuring that there is sufficient capacity for vaccine production.

CHALLENGES IN CRISIS PREVENTION AND MANAGEMENT

The timing, frequency, and extent of a crisis are naturally very uncertain. Certain regularly recurring events can be predicted with some certainty. For example, Europe sees several waves of influenza infections every fall and winter. This is why vaccine production begins months in advance, even though, at that point, the crisis hasn't yet occurred. However, the experience of recent years allows us to estimate the demand for vaccines, and the state guarantees manufacturers a predictable income by assuming vaccination costs as a benefit of statutory health insurance.

The uncertainty is significantly greater during extreme weather events. The probability of occurrence is low, but as climate change continues, it is altering and affecting each region differently. While countries in the Mediterranean region have planned and built their cities knowing that days or weeks of extreme heat can occur in summer, German cities have often been built and developed without considering these risks. In order to adapt the infrastructure to the increasing risk of heat, investments are required in air conditioning, cooling systems, and green corridors, for example. Still, the benefits of these will only be realized in the future.

Even in the ideal case of a state solely concerned with society's long-term well-being, it is challenging in a democratic system to convince the electorate that there should be investment in avoiding crises. On the one hand, this is because, in the case of crises that did not happen, it is not easy to prove that the costs of preventing crises were justified, because without them, it would have been even more expensive. It's hard to show evidence of crises that have been prevented. On the other hand, this is because not everyone would be affected equally by a hypothetical crisis, and the distribution of costs naturally leads to debates.

The situation is exacerbated by the fact that politicians may also pursue their own interests when making decisions. The fact that the costs and benefits of crisis prevention do not happen simultaneously makes it less likely for political and economic reasons that the state will invest sufficiently in crisis prevention that will only benefit the electorate in the future. Policymakers hoping for re-election have greater incentive to consider benefits to the current electorate than to future voters. They will, therefore, give priority to short-term projects over long-term ones.

This is particularly true because parliamentary terms limit the timescale for political decisions.

This dilemma of excessive short-term orientation applies not exclusively to elected politicians. The board members of large companies usually have fixed-term contracts, too. In the private sector, this also means that preventive measures that would be needed are not implemented because they increase costs in the short term, while the long-term benefits are only realized after a delay and only with positive probability.

At the same time, in a democracy, a temporary mandate forces those who hold office to consider the electorate's interests if they are interested in running for re-election. Experiences in dealing with the pandemic, in particular, show that this puts the advantages of a non-democratic state, which some people insist upon, into perspective. Such states indeed have greater power to enforce policies. However, there is a risk that, without feedback from the population, they will use this power to implement measures that even go against the population's interests.

HOW WELL HAS THE STATE FULFILLED ITS ROLE IN THE EVENT OF A CRISIS?

If we now apply the test and ask whether the German state has or will fulfill its job of coordination during the past and current crises, then the results are mixed.

During the pandemic, vaccine development and production could only occur at an accelerated pace because government purchase guarantees ensured the manufacturers' income and the companies could take on the enormous financial risk. The state also protected the population from the uncontrolled spread of the virus by regulating business and school closures when neither any form of immunity had been established nor the health risk fully understood. These decisions were naturally made in situations of great uncertainty and were different in all countries. For an overall assessment, however, the decisive factor is not which decisions were correct in retrospect, but which ones were correct given the level of knowledge at the time of the decision—after weighing up the respective risks. At the same time, the pandemic exposed some administrative weak points, such as the inadequate digitalization of health authorities and poor equipment in and preparation of schools to carry out hybrid teaching.

The energy crisis, in turn, has revealed completely different deficits. When purchasing Russian fuel, the risk assessment carried out by both private and state actors must, in retrospect, be described as simply inadequate. All sides, public and private, depended on Russia as a reliable supplier of natural gas and oil and took no precautions for possible interruptions. On a positive note, the German federal government acted quickly and forcefully as a buyer on the global market, procuring alternatives such as LNG gas and providing the necessary infrastructure by building LNG terminals. However, the state's preparedness for the crisis was made more difficult because components related to energy security, such as gas storage facilities, were privately operated and in Russian ownership, and therefore no information was available about their fill levels. Given the enormous externalities that arise from these system-related components, the lack of state monitoring is a failure. A lack of information about consumption and the needs of end customers has, in turn, impaired the accuracy of policy measures to cushion the burden.

Russia's attack on Ukraine has brought geopolitical risks into greater focus. The Russian attack has led many to reassess the likelihood of future military conflicts, both in Europe and Southeast Asia.

Previously, most private and state actors had classified this risk as rather low. This has now changed. The question is, what consequences will the respective actors draw from this reassessment? This clearly shows the discrepancy between individual and systemic risk. Companies are usually part of increasingly complex supply chains and are exposed to global risks. The overall supply chain is only as resilient as its weakest link, and it is difficult for an individual company to monitor all the risks. State-mandated stress tests, such as those carried out by banks, could reveal these risks, thus ensuring greater risk awareness in companies. At the same time, it is important to avoid systemic crises that arise when many, especially large, companies expose themselves to the same risk, such as concentrating their imports and/or exports on China. Without adequate framework conditions and guidelines, the private sector will not sufficiently take into account the systemic risks arising from individual behavior, which will have negative consequences for other actors who are not directly involved. Security-related aspects may also be assessed differently from the perspective of society as a whole than from the perspective of individual companies. The short-term gain in selling security-related technology to Chinese interested parties conflicts with a state's legitimate security interests and must be assessed politically.

Climate protection as a declared political goal is not a reaction to a short-term crisis phenomenon but is intended to limit long-term climate change and its negative consequences. Climate protection is a public good *par excellence* because the individual's contribution to it incurs individual costs, while everyone benefits from it. Therefore, without government guidelines, there will not be enough climate protection. The government measures to date are primarily aimed at reducing global warming and focus on curbing carbon emissions and transforming the economy and society to do so. Precisely because this is a long-term, global problem, the political and economic issues mentioned above are severe. For political decision-makers, regardless of the country, it is not an attractive option to burden their current population with high carbon prices to reduce carbon dioxide emissions since the advantages of this will primarily benefit subsequent generations—and not only in their own country, but in other countries too. Therefore, it is not surprising that countries worldwide are finding it extremely difficult to implement appropriate measures.

EXTENDING STATE CAPACITY

Whether the state can fulfill the abovementioned tasks depends mainly on state capacity. This term comprises the state's ability to carry out basic functions such as maintaining public order, enforcing laws, collecting taxes, and providing public goods. For the interaction of market actors to function in a capitalist system, the state must create an environment in which economic activities can flourish, while also providing regulations and controls to address market failures and social inequalities.

In past crises, it has become clear in many instances that state administrations were unable—or only to a limited extent—to respond adequately to the changed circumstances and to implement crisis measures promptly. For example, the pandemic restricted the work of the state apparatus itself because hybrid work options were not available, and the necessary data and appropriately trained personnel to enact targeted policy measures were often missing. In some cases, the state did not have the information and capacity to coordinate the actors efficiently in the event of a crisis. Demographic change will make it even more difficult for the state to fulfill these tasks when the baby boomers, who enjoy above-average representation in administrative roles, retire. This means that further capacity is lost.

Various measures are therefore required to strengthen state capacity. Improving public administration and governance must be the top priority. This includes the professionalization and digitalization of public services. Administrative processes must be mapped and digitalized. This is a necessary condition for using new technologies, such as generative artificial intelligence, and integrating them into these processes. And this is the only way the state can make itself an attractive employer for digital natives.

The solution lies partly in the actions of the state and the people themselves. Those responsible often focus on legal certainty and the implementation of proven processes, not on taking risks and having the courage to take responsibility. More complex situations and crises inevitably lead to delayed decisions and, at best, incremental progress. This can have fatal consequences, culminating in loss of control and the breakdown of state coordination, and it costs trust and money.

Strong state capacity also depends on the government's legitimacy, which is achieved through free and fair elections, encouraging citizen participation, and ensuring freedom of expression. To achieve this, it is crucial to consolidate democratic institutions and processes through transparency in government processes and strengthening accountability. The involvement of citizens in decision-making processes and transparency in governance increase trust in the state and its legitimacy. The legitimacy of democratic systems is also strengthened when the representation of all sections of the population is sufficiently guaranteed. Therefore, promoting social inclusion and cohesion is integral to this. Measures to reduce inequality, promote social mobility, and integrate disadvantaged groups into society give these groups confidence that their needs, too, are being taken into account.

Finally, international benchmarking is helpful. Sharing best practices and experiences from other countries can help develop more effective strategies to improve state capacity. This also facilitates harmonization and coordination between states during global crises. Transnational coordination will become increasingly important in a future that is economically, socially, and institutionally imbricated. This also requires state capacity at the international level, which ideally facilitates the work of regional institutions by providing information and a basis for decision-making.

Note

1. Editor's note: The Coase Theorem states that market participants can independently internalize externalities by allocating property rights and subsequent negotiations, so long as property rights are distributed, there are no transaction costs, and there are no information asymmetries.

CHAPTER 10

CLIMATE CHANGE CHANGES EVERYTHING

WOLFGANG SCHÖN

If we are wondering whether our systems will survive the challenges of the coming years, we must also look at how these systems can influence, strengthen, and weaken each other. Democracy and economy, society and politics, science and law—they are all highly interdependent. Education strengthens prosperity and democracy. Democracy strengthens the rule of law and peace. Peace enables growth and culture. Growth and culture enable education. The crisis of our era has justifiably been called a "polycrisis" in which many subsystems of our coexistence are coming under pressure at the same time and are therefore limited in their ability to stabilize each other.

And yet something is different and new. And this different and new thing is climate change and its influence on the entirety of systems in terms of economy, society, and politics. World history—to use a lofty term—has seen the rise and fall of great empires, the shift from democracy to autocracy (or anarchy) and vice versa, as well as a succession of periods of cultural or economic prosperity. But at no time in the recorded history of our planet has a global natural phenomenon shaken in such a short space of time the robust framework within which government, economy, and culture traditionally develop. It's no longer just about the traditional interplay of forces, about the ups and downs of states and cultures. It's about the playing field itself becoming unhinged, being subject to seismic shifts, and becoming completely unreliable.

Today many things are clear: without massive efforts to reduce the global economy's carbon emissions, the Earth's atmosphere will quickly warm up beyond the critical thresholds of 1.5°C or 2°C above historical temperatures. The consequences are predictable: rising sea levels causing flooding across large areas of the land, massive droughts and weather catastrophes, the spread of tropical diseases, and much more.

Human coexistence will be comprehensively affected: global migratory movements will intensify, economic inequality will grow, and conflicts over raw materials, food, and access to medical care will increase.

What is crucial for our issue now is that the "climate problem" cannot be viewed or solved in isolation from the stability of the other subsystems—and vice versa. Rather, global changes in climate will have significant effects on all other areas of human life. Climate-related migration will increase the challenges of migratory movements that have already been triggered by wars and poverty and are associated with considerable social tensions. Climate-related diseases will increase pressure on the provision of medical services to the world's population. Climate-related impoverishment will further strain social cohesion within states and at the global level. In other words, if the climate system is not repaired, all other systems might also lose their functionality. And that also means that the old strategies used by Western industrialized countries to create economic growth and social balance no longer work.

However, the attempt to stabilize the climate system can only succeed (and this is also a truism today) if all (or at least a majority) of the world's countries are prepared to make a joint effort. No country can make a substantial contribution to this on its own. This is the desire of the arduous COP conferences, of the European Union's far-reaching environmental activities, and of the attempts to establish a strong "climate club" of the most important emitting states.

However, this is precisely where the challenges of the climate system come into conflict (a conflict that's not absolutely essential, but real nevertheless) with the developments of other systems in the areas of politics, economics, and culture. One obvious example of this is climate-related migration, which will intensify the already increasing tendency towards isolation on the part of the "rich" states and thus produce conflict rather than cooperation. Another example is the global expansion of social and economic inequality caused by floods and droughts, including the impact on agricultural production. Although the first agreements were reached at the COP28 summit for a global "climate fund" to benefit poorer countries, offsetting emissions-related damage, we are still a long way from a real leveling up.

The need to combat climate change using globally coordinated strategies ultimately stands in fundamental contrast to the growing fragmentation of the world of states and to an intensifying conflict between democratically governed states in the Western world on the one hand and autocratic systems in Russia and the People's Republic of China on the other. The Global South also sees itself in distinct opposition to the traditional industrialized states, an opposition that is stoked not only by current economic imbalances, but also by the colonial past of many Western nations. So how is it possible for the United States, the European Union, Russia, China, and India, as the main producers of carbon emissions, to reach an agreement on climate policy when at the same time they find each other on different sides of the war in Ukraine? In such a global situation, can the necessary trust arise between the actors, and can mutual obligations be observed and enforced?

It is not least regional and domestic political tensions that conflict with global climate policy requirements. Germany's energy policy over the last few years is an outstanding example of this. During Angela Merkel's term as Chancellor, the federal government had already initiated its unilateral abandonment of both nuclear energy and coal-fired power generation (for reasons that were justifiable, although not entirely convincing). Given the low availability of renewable energy sources, in retrospect this necessarily led to a high level of dependence on the so-called "bridge technology" of natural gas generation and thus in turn to close economic ties with Russia as a supplier of cheap energy. The dispute over the Nord Stream 2 pipeline is the best-known symbol of this. Under Germany's "traffic light" coalition government,[1] environmental policy requirements were tightened after 2021, and the expansion of electric mobility and electric heat pumps for buildings accelerated in the hope that in future the electricity required would largely be provided via environmentally friendly production. With Russia's attack on Ukraine, this strategy collapsed for the time being. Initially, access to Russian gas was cut off by political means and in part also by technical means. Germany's federal government was faced with the tricky dilemma of either allowing the nuclear power plants to run for a longer period of time or returning to coal-fired power—or buying gas on the world markets at a high price and thus to the detriment of the domestic economy. The German people began to feel the effects of both climate policy and the war in Ukraine on their energy costs and reacted angrily. Suddenly the energy crisis was transformed into a possible driver of social conflicts in addition to its economic effects on Germany as a location for energy-intensive industrial production. The federal government reacted instinctively with price subsidies and tax relief, but this strategy came to an end at the latest with the budget ruling of the Federal Constitutional Court in November 2023, which forced the government in Berlin to account honestly for the costs of its energy policy over recent years.[2]

The long-term effects of these developments in the energy sector cannot yet be foreseen. France and other European and non-European countries are once again emphasizing and strengthening their nuclear energy supply option, thereby running contrary to the German federal government. In the US, the ecological transformation is being driven forward by the Biden government's massive, debt-supported, and therefore unsustainable policy of subsidies. This will also create a trade conflict with the European Union, which could intensify further after the US presidential elections in November 2024. To finance the war in Ukraine, Russia is now exporting its oil and gas to the states of the Global South, where new alliances appear to be forming (as clearly demonstrated by the forced withdrawal of France and Germany from several North African states).

The need to address these cumulative systemic disruptions all at the same time makes many democratic states appear overwhelmed at first glance. Not only in Germany, but also in France, the United Kingdom and many other countries in the Western world, governments are exposed to a difficult to resolve and seemingly constant conflict between environmental policy, economic policy, and social policy to foreign and defense policy. This may give the impression of a lack of strategic ability and sometimes even of helplessness on the part of the actors. And yet anyone who considers the political assertiveness of autocratic or even dictatorial systems to be an advantage in the current world situation would be mistaken. Nowhere in the world is ecological balance so disregarded as in dictatorships or systems under populist control (just think of the Bolsonaro government's treatment of the Brazilian rainforest). Dictators too want to please their people. And ultimately, it's the dictatorships that prefer external, if not military, conflict to global cooperation in order to secure a free hand in domestic politics. Russia's attack on Ukraine is just one striking example of this. We need hardly mention that such military conflicts always also cause massive, long-term environmental damage.

But back to climate change. It is one of the truisms of the climate policy debate that the global emission reductions required will be very costly. Existing production facilities must be closed or converted. Significant investments are needed to find new energy sources. The loss of prosperity will be partly temporary, but partly permanent. It is the task of governments to organize the allocation of these losses in prosperity between states, but also within these states. And at this point there is no way of avoiding intervention in the other systems, namely economic and social systems. This requires significant consensus from governments around the world, but these governments also need major consensus within their national communities.

And this consensus is largely absent—even in Germany. Disputes over the actions of activists such as "The Last Generation" and "Just Stop Oil" have shown two things: on the one hand, the willingness of environmental activists to increase their influence and visibility through the use of illegal methods has become noticeable. On the other hand—and this is perhaps the most regrettable aspect of these actions—the "climate critics" suddenly saw themselves as legitimized. Understandably rejecting this type of protest, at the same time they reject the need for a climate-oriented policy as a whole or at least push it into the background. Germany's climate policy consensus, which was still within easy reach in the election year of 2021, appears to have largely disappeared at the start of 2024. The sometimes unfortunate regulatory approaches of the "traffic light" government have contributed to climate opponents' claim to be defending the freedom of the individual against an "eco-dictatorship."

This pseudo-liberal approach will not help us. Combating climate change not only requires a global consensus among states, but also a conscious, albeit limited, renunciation of freedom and prosperity on the part of the individual. Anyone who fundamentally rejects this will be responsible for the lasting consequences of a failed reform of the climate system for the other systems in society, the economy, and politics. Such people will defend the ability to travel freely on German freeways, but in doing so will promote climate migration. Are these the right value decisions?

What is the conclusion? What applies to the world's climate applies literally to the health of the individual: a healthy climate isn't everything, but everything is nothing without a healthy climate. Only if we succeed in stabilizing the global climate system will we have a chance of maintaining the resilience of our other systems.

Notes

1. Editor's note: In German politics, a "traffic light" coalition government is made up of the Social Democratic Party (SPD), the Free Democratic Party (FDP), and the Greens.

2. In 2021 the German government transferred debt raised to help the country cope with COVID-19 to a climate fund to try to make the most of a temporary suspension of borrowing limits in the constitution. However, in November 2023 the Constitutional Court ruled that this move was incompatible with the debt brake enshrined in Germany's Basic Law and so was void, thus creating a €60-billion budget shortfall.

CHAPTER 11

ECONOMIC DEVELOPMENT AND SUSTAINABILITY

CLEMENS FUEST

I. INTRODUCTION: WHAT IS THE RELATIONSHIP BETWEEN ECONOMIC GROWTH AND SUSTAINABILITY?

The relationship between economic development and ecological sustainability is one of the most urgent issues of our time. Debates on this subject often emphasize the suggestion that a conflict exists between sustainability and economic prosperity. This is not really a convincing argument as any destruction of the natural environment will sooner or later adversely impact economic prosperity too. At the same time, it is true that protecting the natural environment takes up resources and may require giving up certain kinds of consumption.

In recent decades, economic growth driven by economic liberalization and globalization has enabled billions of people to lead prosperous lives and has reduced global poverty. However, this positive development has been accompanied by excessive environmental pollution and an erosion of the natural necessities of existence. Economic growth at the expense of the environment has its limits. Natural resources also have important economic functions. In the long term, economic prosperity will only be possible if the overexploitation of nature is ended. From this perspective, economic and ecological sustainability are not a contradiction, but rather two sides of the same coin.

Global warming lies at the heart of the debate about ecological sustainability. Despite all the appeals for more climate protection, global greenhouse gas emissions continue to rise every year. They have increased by around a third since the year 2000, and there is no end in sight to the rise. But climate change is not the only, perhaps not even the most urgent, environmental problem. At least as dramatic is the global decline in biodiversity. Today people and livestock make up 96 percent of all mammals in the world.[1] Animals in the wild represent only 4 percent of the population. The number of insects and birds has also been falling for years. Deforestation plays an important role in both global warming and the decline in biodiversity. The destruction of tropical rainforests, especially in the Amazon basin, is particularly serious. These forests are home to a large proportion of the world's animal and plant species. They are of vital importance in the fight to stop global warming. However, it has not yet been possible to halt the destruction of the tropical rainforests.

This ongoing environmental destruction is problematic for many reasons. But as we already mentioned, it is also highly damaging from a purely economic perspective. How can it be made clear that protecting the environment and maintaining economic prosperity are not mutually contradictory? The British economist Partha Dasgupta argues that a healthy environment can be viewed as a form of capital that produces valuable services, similar to human-made capital in the form of machines or houses.[2] The most accessible and frequently cited example is the pollination of flowers by bees. Food production through fishing and agriculture, the extraction of groundwater, the absorption of CO_2, the provision of recreational areas for people and, last but not least, protection against epidemics and other health risks are other indispensable services performed by this natural capital. From this perspective, sustainable economic activity means maintaining natural capital and thus the supply of these essential services and securing them for the future.

II. SUSTAINABILITY FROM AN ECONOMIC POINT OF VIEW: THE DASGUPTA MODEL

Partha Dasgupta's analysis of economic development and sustainability is useful for two main reasons. First, it makes it clear that there are valid economic reasons to halt the destruction of nature. Second, it creates a consistent and manageable framework for the highly diverse and complex problem of sustainability. Of course, the price for doing this is that the analysis abstracts from lots of details. However, it does create an overall picture of the problem that can be interpreted meaningfully. Dasgupta sees intact nature as capital that provides valuable services but erodes when over-consumed. In this model, natural capital has properties that are very similar to human capital or physical capital. However, it can only be replaced by human or physical capital to a very limited extent. If one assumes that economic growth in the form of the production of goods and services is accompanied by a certain demand on natural resources and that this "natural consumption" exceeds the level that is compensated for by natural regeneration, then such development is unsustainable. Sustainability means reducing the demand on natural resources.

To understand the idea of preserving natural capital as a concept of sustainability, it is helpful to draw on a simplified version of the Dasgupta model, that is viewing natural resources as a stock of capital that produces services, capital such as forests, oceans, lakes, populations of wild animals, raw materials, land, and so on. This capital has a natural ability to regenerate. A certain amount of demand is therefore possible without eroding the stock. However, this ability to regenerate is limited. When natural capital is over-consumed, the supply decreases. Sustainability requires stabilization of the stock of natural capital. The demand on natural capital is a consequence of the production of goods and services. This consumption is also known as *ecological footprint*. The greater the stock of natural capital, the more services it can produce without over-consumption. Conversely, constant over-consumption causes natural capital to erode at an increasing rate. The stock of natural capital can also be increased through direct investments that build up this capital, such as reforestation or carbon capture and storage (CCS).

Sustainable development means that natural capital must not shrink constantly but is at least maintained. In order to achieve this, the ecological footprint, i.e., the consumption of natural capital, must not exceed this capital's natural capacity for regeneration.[3] According to estimates by the Global Footprint Network, the current global ecological footprint is 1.7, i.e., 170 percent of what would be compatible with maintaining natural capital. These estimates are methodologically tricky and the results controversial. We cannot rule out the possibility that they are overestimating the problem; but they might also be underestimating it. Let's assume the value of 1.7 is correct. What changes would be needed to achieve sustainable development? In the case of a given gross domestic product, the efficiency of our economy in terms of the consumption of natural resources per unit of gross domestic product[4] would have to improve massively. Today we should only be using two thirds of what we are currently consuming, in which case the ecological footprint would equal one, and no more natural capital would be consumed than what would grow back through natural regeneration. This applies worldwide.

However, this increase in efficiency takes time. Meanwhile, the economy continues to grow, with a corresponding consumption of natural resources. It is therefore inevitable that natural capital will continue to shrink, at least for a transitional period, even with increased efforts to protect nature. Therefore, improvements needed to achieve sustainability in the form of reducing the consumption of natural resources through economic activity are significantly greater. It is assumed that it will take ten years before efforts at environmental protection and technical innovations reduce global environmental consumption to a sustainable level. According to a rough calculation, environmental consumption per unit of economic output would have to reduce to around one third of the current level of consumption within this period.

There may be differing opinions as to whether a reduction in environmental consumption to this extent is achievable. What are the options remaining if that doesn't work? We can take more time, but then the increase in efficiency must be even greater. Another option is investing more in natural capital, in which case we can get by with smaller increases in efficiency. In any case, it is clear that preserving the natural environment and thus the transition to sustainable economic activity requires considerable effort.

How can we achieve such a transformation? First, this requires a convincing measurement of natural capital and appropriate communication strategies. Second, we need technical innovations in order to reduce the consumption of natural capital caused by the production of goods and services.[5] This includes converting energy supply to climate-neutral technologies as well as the production of fully recyclable cars and other machines, and much more. Third, advances and innovations in the organization of economic and social processes are important. This includes better monitoring and enforcement of environmental protection regulations, but also an intelligent environmental protection policy; for example, tradable certificates for greenhouse gas emissions, which avoid unnecessary cost burdens.[6] Fourth, in addition to innovations, we need direct investments in natural capital; for example, the aforementioned reforestation and the designation of nature reserves. The protection of the remaining tropical rainforests is of paramount importance.

III. DEGROWTH AS THE SOLUTION?

Another approach to reducing the ecological footprint, which is much discussed, would be to reduce the global gross domestic product or at least forgo further growth.[7] This is the route favored by the so-called "degrowth movement."

This requirement raises significant problems. Above all, economic growth is a factor that is not directly controllable by governments, but rather is the result of the free activity of billions of people. Of course governments could try to reduce economic output through state intervention. In principle, there are already a number of state interventions that reduce economic growth, often unintentionally. However, it is questionable whether a reduction in economic output could and should be the long-term goal of government policy. People in developing and emerging countries in particular will not give up the opportunity to achieve greater prosperity, and it is also morally dubious to ask for this.

Even in high-income countries such as Germany, a policy of contraction will find little political support. In addition, the willingness to use resources for environmental protection tends to decrease when material prosperity declines. If people voluntarily give up consumption that pollutes the environment through a change in consciousness or education, that is something different. However, such behavioral changes have so far been the exception. Therefore, focusing technical and social progress on environmental protection, combined with investments in the regeneration and preservation of natural capital, is the more promising route to sustainability.

IV. DOES SUSTAINABLE DEVELOPMENT FAIL BECAUSE OF GOVERNANCE PROBLEMS?

The idea that a move towards greater sustainability in the economy and society is desirable and necessary undoubtedly enjoys great support in many countries and among the majority of the population. However, there are significant hurdles to implementing this idea. On the one hand, there are diverging opinions about how quickly and with which tools sustainability issues should be pursued. One particularly fraught question is which social groups should bear which burdens. In addition, efforts to increase sustainability represent investments whose benefits lie in the future, while political and sometimes private-sector decision-making processes are often more oriented to the short term.

Achieving a move towards sustainable economic activity is also difficult because decisions about environmental protection are made primarily by national governments that have limited incentives to take on costs for environmental protection themselves if the benefits are enjoyed at a global level. Nevertheless, highly developed countries such as Germany can still contribute by participating in international agreements for climate and environmental protection. It is also important to develop environmentally friendly technical solutions that are attractive regardless of their environmental impact and can therefore also be adopted by countries where problems other than ecological sustainability are given priority.

Making progress in solving sustainability problems that require international cooperation is particularly challenging. This applies, for example, to international or global environmental problems such as climate protection or the protection of the world's oceans. It may be rational for each individual country to do nothing in this context or simply to invest in adapting to environmental problems. Collectively, however, this kind of attitude leads to a poor outcome. Even if a willingness to cooperate globally exists, the question of how to deal with sustainability problems still needs to be resolved. The Dasgupta model says that, in principle, both giving up production or consumption and improving efficiency, i.e., reducing the consumption of natural capital per unit of economic output, are conceivable routes. Investments in natural capital can also contribute. The issue of which combination of these options should be chosen is highly controversial. In principle, it is possible for politics to forgo making a decision about this issue and limit themselves to creating regulations that are necessary for sustainability. In this case, adaptation results automatically through a particular combination of reduced consumption and technical innovation. This adaptation would be optimal if there is no market failure when making the relevant decisions—invest more in innovation or consume less.

One example of this is the European system of tradable CO_2 certificates (Emissions Trading Scheme). Whether companies and private households adapt to this by decarbonizing economic activity through innovations or by phasing out economic activity that is associated with CO_2 emissions can be left to the market.

This is not to say that government policy to encourage climate protection should be limited to setting a framework of tradable certificates. For example, research and development in decarbonization results in positive externalities. This is an argument in favor of state support for innovation. When it comes to future CO_2 prices, problems of political credibility can lead to private investors investing too little in decarbonization. State support may also be required here. However, all of this does not mean that the state has to specify to what extent innovation and to what extent less production should contribute to reducing emissions. The same applies to environmental protection in other areas. What is crucial is achieving the goals of sustainability.

Notes

1. Our World in Data, "Wild mammals make up only a few percent of the world's mammals," December 15, 2022, https://ourworldindata.org/wild-mammals-birds-biomass (accessed January 8, 2024).

2. Partha Dasgupta, *The Economics of Biodiversity: The Dasgupta Review* (London: HM Treasury, 2021).

3. Assume that the following linear relationship, F=YN/A, exists between the production of goods and services per year and per capita of the population (Y), the population size (N) and the ecological footprint (F). A is a parameter that describes the extent to which production consumes natural resources. The value of A reflects the status of the

production technology used and the organization of the economy. The ability of natural capital (K) to produce services without shrinking is described by the function S (K). S is an increasing function of K. The stock of natural capital can also be increased through direct investments (I) in the growth of this capital, such as reforestation or carbon capture and storage (CCS). Within this framework, there is only one condition for sustainability which can be formulated as:

$$YN/A = S(K) + I$$

This equation states that the annual consumption of natural capital does not exceed the growth, i.e.,

the sum of natural regeneration and investments in natural capital.

4. In the equation (see Note 3) this is represented by parameter A.

5. In the equation (see Note 3) this would correspond to an increase in the technology parameter A. The higher A becomes, the lower the ecological footprint per unit of economic output.

6. In the equation (see Note 3) this aspect is also contained within parameter A.

7. In the equation (see Note 3) this would be the ecological footprint shrinking through a reduction of YN.

CHAPTER 12

TRANSFORM YOURSELF

TIMO MEYNHARDT

Marina (24) could hardly believe it. It came as an unpleasant surprise to her when she held the results of her leadership test in her hands. As a future leader, she was firmly convinced that she wanted to do the right thing: work for the success of the company while serving the common good. She is committed to greater justice and more climate protection and believes in responsible entrepreneurship. She is also toying with the idea of founding a start-up herself.

But the analysis of her basic orientations[1] is giving her food for thought. First of all, effective action, combined with a great sense of responsibility, is particularly important to Marina. She wants to do the right thing in a responsible way. In this part of the evaluation, she can recognize herself. However, she is very concerned by the surprisingly low orientation towards the common good (Purpose). On the other hand, she's less worried by the somewhat average orientation towards Entrepreneurial spirit. Marina looks at the questions again carefully. It's true that when weighing up the possible answers, she's rarely chosen to focus on social benefits and has set her passion for social issues aside in favor of other answers. But why? She can't stop going over it in her mind.

Marina listens attentively to the following lecture on the Leipzig Leadership Model[2] and writes down verbatim: "Good leadership begins with the willingness to question yourself all the time, and to recognize your own inner contradictions as a source of change and new ideas." She doesn't know exactly what that might mean, but this much is clear—there's a lot of work ahead of her.

NO "NEW NORMAL" IN SIGHT

Marina follows the news closely and reads much more than just the business press. She is aware of how species extinction, extreme weather events, and melting glaciers are linked to global warming. She has now also read the *Earth for All* report[3] and knows why scientists are talking about the Anthropocene, the age of human impact on Earth. For the first time in human history, people's behavior is threatening their own environmental conditions on Earth. Marina was really affected by the report. Now she understands the urgency of switching to renewable energies and re-thinking lots of other things. But she still lacks a sense of what the consequences of new concepts of mobility and housing, for example, might be for the economy and society. Marina is following the debates at the 2023 UN Climate Change Conference in Dubai with great interest. She thinks that the wording in the final report that talks about "transitioning away from fossil fuels"[4] seems too weak, but it's something. She is surprised that this was the 28th conference of this kind. Before, she didn't listen so closely. Marina is increasingly wondering how leaders should orient themselves in this state of chaos. Now she remembers that, without much thought, she had volunteered when she was asked in the lecture who among those present would like to become a future leader. She stands by that.

The professor continues her lecture: "In a time of overlapping crises, leaders face major challenges, and some are even overwhelmed. It's not surprising that concepts such as 'resilience' and 'future skills' are popular. How do we achieve energy transition without backing the wrong horse? What impact do new global military conflicts have on our trade relations? In what ways do we have to rely on artificial intelligence in order to keep pace? And all of this is taking place in an environment of political conflicts in which we increasingly expect clear positioning from private business." In the subsequent group discussion Marina and her fellow students repeatedly return to the question of what the real focus should be. She hopes to get a lot of new ideas from her studies. Surely there must be something other than the Net Present Value method, competitive advantages, and scarcity problems.

Then the professor starts talking again and, somewhat stressed, says that it is completely hopeless to address these questions using just an economic risk analysis that refers to existing knowledge. And she continues that we must face up to the fact that if you're not looking for (new) orientation today you're not up to speed. For her, today's challenges are like Gordian knots that can neither be easily cut nor skillfully untangled. Driven by the overwhelming climate crisis, we are at the beginning of a huge transformation process in both economy and society, the extent of which we and later generations will probably only become aware of in retrospect. As attractive as a "social contract for a great transformation"[5] may seem, says the professor, there is no social consensus in sight. In a pluralistic, open society, centrally controlled mechanisms for collective decision-making are becoming less and less realistic. Only the constant feedback provided by social media creates a different kind of framework for communication.

Marina is somewhat reassured by these statements because it seems that others too sense a general uncertainty and are looking for new ways forward. She's also interested in historical accounts that make comparisons with other "great transformations"[6] in human history. The new factor is the time pressure triggered by changes in the stability of the Earth's system. For example, there was no external pressure to act caused by climate change in the case of the transition from a hunter-gatherer society to the spread of settlements (the Neolithic Revolution) or in the switch to a regime of fossil fuels (the Industrial Revolution). Today, the measurable breach of planetary boundaries[7] might require both economy and society to adapt in ways that cannot be postponed in order to preserve human livelihoods in their current form. We can only guess at the extent of this. Given the possible consequences of global warming, Marina no longer thinks that the notion of a necessary "socio-ecological transformation"[8] is overstated.

TRANSFORMATION IS A CHANGE OF STATE

Marina can hardly keep up with her note-taking in lectures. The current renaissance of the concept of transformation can be understood as expressing a desire to shape things in the face of climate change. The challenge is huge. How can you actively bring about change in a complex system without providing a more detailed description of the target state? It's like a race: as a society we have to transform ourselves faster than the Earth's system is transforming itself. Since humans became a dominant, influencing factor, maintaining current living conditions on Earth is at risk. It's about focused change, in which our ability to consciously shape is clearly limited. Conflicts, non-simultaneous developments, and counter-movements characterize the contradictory nature of all transformation processes.

By visualizing a ball,[9] Marina now understands for the first time what could be meant by a tipping point and the idea of planetary boundaries.[10] A ball lies in a valley. It is occasionally pushed from outside, but it always rolls back to the lowest point. Everything stays more or less the same. There is a dynamic balance. However, if the forces of transformation are greater than the forces of inertia, or the bottom of the valley flattens out, then the ball no longer returns to its starting point. The previous inertia of the ball turns out to be deceptive, and now its behavior is no longer predictable. If it exceeds a critical point, then lots of things are possible, just not a return to the previous state. Does the ball find a new equilibrium in a different valley, or does it swing back and forth between different new states? Or will everything end in chaos?

As Marina tries to follow these arguments, her thoughts keep wandering. For example, she remembers the wording on the cover of an issue of *McKinsey Quarterly*: "Transformation—Reimagining the top line, the bottom line and everything in between."[11] From now on she will look for clues as to what this means in all her lectures. Will valuation models for companies change? For a long time Marina has been interested in climate finance, as well as new forms of ownership and the circular economy. Marina has already read everything she could about doughnut economics[12] and leadership in the Anthropocene.[13] She is worried, but doesn't want to fall victim to climate fear[14] and rejects protests such as gluing yourself to things or throwing paint over works of art. Marina wants to make a contribution, get involved, and take responsibility.

IT ALL STARTS WITH A FEELING OF UNEASE

Marina latches onto one of the professor's last comments before the break: "This new approach to the world involves a different approach to ourselves. Both are closely linked and mutually dependent. On the one hand, we have to react and adapt to the changes in our environment. On the other hand—and this applies to leaders in particular—we are called upon to actively shape this transformative change and lead the way. To do this, we must first question our own understanding. Fear and doubt are good advisors in such situations because they make us physically feel that the previous order of things is no longer sustainable. We notice this because dealing with the challenges saps our strength. We lose the basic feeling of being able to make a difference, or worse, we lose confidence in ourselves. In retrospect, such insecurity might have been the price we pay for true self-development. But we can't know this in advance, we have to believe in it." That sounds familiar, thinks Marina. Is the image of the ball in the valley relevant here too?

Finally it's break time. Marina excitedly tells her friend about a book she's recently discovered. It's called *Land Sickness*[15] and was written by Nikolaj Schultz, a Danish sociologist who is of an age to be her older brother. This book too starts with a feeling of unease. Whether it's the energy consumed when using an electric fan, the supermarket plastic bags polluting the oceans, or the soil destruction that results from avocado-farming—in these and many other of his actions, the book's protagonist sees himself as deeply involved in all the negative effects human lifestyles have on the environment. Isn't he exaggerating a little when he writes: "Every day, I realize that the problem is *me*"?[16] Yes and no. Of course the individual can only do so much. The big levers lie somewhere else entirely—in industry and to a different extent from country to country. Marina knows all of this, but it seems less and less an excuse for her to do nothing. At least it doesn't calm her down. What really startled her was the sentence: "It seems the Anthropocene is not a nice place to sleep."[17]

Marina devoured the book and then read it a second time. It wasn't necessarily the story itself that triggered something in her. The story itself is quickly summarized: a young man living in Paris struggles with the realization that his way of life is contributing to the global climate crisis. Due to the extreme heat in the city, he goes on a sailing trip with friends to an island in the Mediterranean. Along the way he makes observations, arrives at new beliefs and, at the end of the fictional story, develops a new mental horizon, based on the image of a journey on the open sea.

The title *Land Sickness* refers to the feeling of dizziness that has gripped the young man because, in times when climate change is threatening, he is finding it increasingly difficult to manage in his search for the right way to live. Marina feels this speaks to her directly and feels challenged to a certain extent. It's immediately clear to her that we have to rethink what it means to be free when climate change imposes unprecedented restrictions on us and our way of life becomes less free. She doesn't feel at all "land sick," but she also has this vague sense that something is wrong and she gets dizzy when she thinks that no one knows exactly how threatening climate change really is.

We can't run away from the problems—after all, running away is not a solution. However, Marina notices in herself and her lifestyle that giving up and moderating her demands doesn't really work. Who does the book's protagonist, a child of affluence, think he is? He can afford to go on a sailing trip because Paris is so hot and an island in the sea offers a way of cooling down. What does he know about the struggle for survival of the world's poor or the daily challenges faced by entrepreneurs?

So Marina reads the chapter called "Freedoms" particularly closely. What does the author think he's doing not distancing himself from nature and questioning today's boundaries? She understands that of course we have to develop a new understanding of freedom, but not like this! Isn't it a real achievement that people have become increasingly independent of the forces of nature, have emancipated themselves from them, and so have gained and should continue to gain more freedom in the way they live their lives?

Marina quickly realizes that the author is thinking more deeply and is looking for a different approach to the world. It can't be a retreat to an inner freedom either: she finds that interesting because she's realized how caught up she is in the problems and so also feels unfree. Marina underlines the following sentence: "If I want my freedom to return, it must be through practicing and cultivating links or relations with all the humans and non-humans that allow for an unfolding experience of self-determination and a sort of hetero-autonomy."[18] Until now she had always thought that freedom was something that had to be negotiated between people. Marina finds it interesting to think that she could feel freer if she viewed dealing with a wide variety of earthly beings around her as a kind of negotiation process. Marina is impressed: finally, a positive thought, completely different from the negative mood created by scenarios of fear. This change of perspective has a liberating effect on her and gives her renewed energy. She tries out an idea: how would it be to see dependence on nature as an opportunity to become more connected to all living things? But obviously it's also about the things that surround us, i.e. the water and the soil. Okay, now that seems a little too romantic to her, but somehow appealing, nevertheless. Didn't previous generations have a different relationship with nature from what we have today? Why shouldn't that work for us?

Now Marina realizes why in the first lecture she was so concerned by the fact that her orientation towards the common good was said to be so low. Until now she thought that the common good was a really big thing that she couldn't influence anyway. After *Land Sickness* she sees things differently. Although she still doesn't know what "hetero-autonomy" means, she is more aware than ever that self-determination isn't just a question of creating boundaries and independence. This is her understanding: we should work towards what unites us in difference. Only the feeling of connection with others and with the environment creates freedom. Marina struggles with the idea that a recognized and consciously chosen dependency should ultimately make her more independent. In any event, it seems very Western and very cerebral to her. Intuitively, she feels that every change in her perspective must feel *natural* to her despite everything, and going too far can be detrimental in other ways. But Marina has understood one thing: her lifestyle makes her part of the problem. However, she can look for ways out and make progress in doing so. Where there is difference there should be connection, as Marina confidently notes.

FROM REFLECTION TO ACTION IN THE ANTHROPOCENE

Maybe that's what the professor meant when she said in her lecture that every external transformation is linked to inner work. She said that each of us has to work with our own strengths and weaknesses in order to take the next step as an individual. One important technique in leadership of oneself, she continued, is the ability to feel conflicts and contradictions deeply and then to be able to take action not as a knee-jerk reaction, but by taking a step back and regaining balance through distance from oneself, that is not despairing and giving up. Does the professor take this on board personally?

In any case, Marina is very proud of her notes on the question posed by the lecture as to what transformation might mean: by transformation we mean the process of change over a longer period of time that leads to a significant change in existing processes, behaviors, or paradigms. It can refer to a gradual or sudden change in current structures and is often accompanied by periods of transition and uncertainty.

We all tend to avoid an overly harsh confrontation with our blind spots, our dark sides, or bad compromises. We repress, project onto others, or look for other self-serving ways of interpreting our own behavior. Protecting our self-esteem in this way is understandable and often necessary in order to create a stable self-image and remain able to act. Depending on our life situation, we are all open to welcoming new things and redefining boundaries to varying extents. But this is exactly what is needed for self-transformation. Marina was aware that her changing view of things was not yet a transformation, but perhaps it was a very personal tipping point. A start seems to have been made.

In contrast to a change within a structure or a process, this involves an aspiration for more and different things. We break away from previous beliefs and develop new attitudes towards ourselves and others—in the best-case scenario, this leads to new behaviors. All of this is most productive when the individual develops as a person alongside their environment and in doing so changes the environment itself.

As a student at a business school, Marina immediately thinks like an entrepreneur. So, what could it mean if we learned to see such basic everyday actions as eating, drinking, sleeping, and working in a different light? It occurs to her that there are already a lot of new business models that rely not just on prevention, but on new ways of dealing with resources, with other people and, last but not least, with ourselves and our bodies.

Although at the beginning of the lecture on the Leipzig Leadership Model[19] she had found the Model really abstract, she could now engage with the basic idea of testing her ideas and decisions using four questions:

- Are we pursuing an overarching goal? (Purpose)

- Are we thinking and acting in an entrepreneurial way? (Entrepreneurial spirit)

- Are our activities legitimate? (Responsibility)

- Are we effective? (Effectiveness)

For Marina, a purpose means contributing to socio-ecological transformation in an entrepreneurial way. This is legitimate given the impact of climate change on humanity as a whole, but especially on those who have to bear the burden most. And of course decisions should not be guided by opinions, but by facts. She now sees more clearly than before the need to place her own actions in a wider context and to see herself as part of it. Where do I get involved? What absolutely needs to be done? Where do I run the risk of ultimately contributing to the stabilization of old patterns of action with supposedly new solutions, even preventing progress? (Fig. 1)

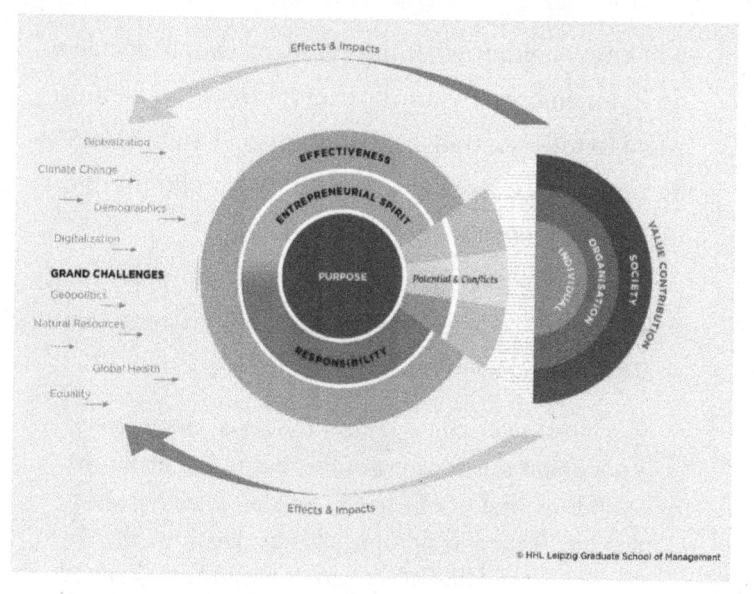

Fig. 1 *The Expanded Leipzig Leadership Model*[20]

A VERY PERSONAL TIPPING POINT

What did the professor say? "The Leipzig Leadership Model created a framework to reflect potentials and tensions in leadership and to develop new perspectives. The answers to these basic questions are of fundamental, even existential importance for a company in times of crisis. Anyone who has not developed an attractive statement about the why and wherefore (Purpose) of their products and services will know neither what the company should decide to do in an emergency nor how employees can be motivated to follow a transformation plan. This problem is becoming even more acute under the conditions of the increasingly prominent climate crisis."

Marina is sure she has understood something. Asked to record her own insights in a learning diary, she writes at the end of the lecture:

> The most important question for me at the moment is not about the meaning of life, but rather about the conditions under which life on this planet is even possible. If these conditions change, we must change too. My life and that of the people around me depends on whether we just keep going until we can't carry on, or whether we engage in a learning process about how to mitigate the consequences of climate change and, above all, how we make progress in so doing.
>
> I have to find ways to relate differently, and in new ways, to the various dependencies in my life. I want to understand how I can influence them and how I am influenced by them. Nikolaj Schultz's ideas opened my eyes to this. I have realized that I am not powerless. I found it exciting to think that in everything I do, I carry both the problem and the solution within me. My individual well-being and the common good are interdependent, in a sense existentially intertwined, and fundamentally inseparable. We live within a system and live by drawing upon a system. This is my area of creative freedom!

I think I would answer the questions in the leadership test differently now. It's still important to me to act effectively and achieve results. However, I now see my entrepreneurial orientation as being much less focused on solving something better than others using a new idea or on mastering a process better. For me, being an entrepreneur now means—like a kind of diplomat—looking for, recognizing, and cultivating connections and dependencies between me and my environment, without elevating myself above other people or things. I hope that by respecting others and those around me I will gain more self-respect. Maybe this is a way to become freer inside and get to know myself better. It's the responsible thing to let others take part and perhaps even implement this in an entrepreneurial way. As I write this, I feel a sense of optimism because I realize how I could use my inner reorganization for the common good. Maybe one day I'll write a book: *The Reinvention of the 'I' in the Anthropocene*.

***

This is how I might imagine the uncertainty students feel when they try to form their own picture of the world in an era of climate change. Because ultimately, after completing their studies, they should take responsibility not only for themselves, but also for others. But this is also how I imagine the path that students can take together with their teachers, and that we can all take if we want to emerge from our feeling of unease and try to make progress by being open to new things. In the case I have described, a changed relationship between the self and the world leads to entrepreneurial action and does not remain trapped in theory. What I have outlined here is of course idealistically magnified. But at the same time, it clarifies a basic aspect of transformational learning: we don't just learn something new; we change our perspective beyond what we previously thought. That's why we talk about *trans*-formation.

As a university lecturer in management studies, I believe that I can provide important insights into how societies, markets, organizations, and companies function, and that I am always up to date with the latest theoretical developments. Yes, this confidence is part of the job. But is this how we as teachers can really encourage transformational learning? It seems to me that instead we should be expressing our own doubts and encouraging critical thinking. Because I too am alarmed when in the lecture hall I say sentences such as these: "The socio-ecological transformation is about nothing less than a complete move away from fossil fuels in our energy systems. This represents a transformative change in business and society, the effects of which no one can estimate. We are not well prepared for this."

The next few years are going to be tough…

Notes

1. Timo Meynhardt, Josephina Steuber, and Max Feser, "The Leipzig Leadership Model: Measuring Leadership Orientations" in *Current Psychology* (2023), pp. 1–20.

2. Timo Meynhardt, Manfred Kirchgeorg, Andreas Pinkwart, Andreas Suchanek, and Henning Zülch (eds.), *Führen in der Krise. Herausforderungen an das Leipziger Führungsmodell* (Leipzig: HHL Academic Press, 2022).

3. Sandrine Dixson-Declève, Owen Gaffney, Jayati Ghosh, Jorgen Randers, and Johan Rockström, *Earth for All. A Survival Guide for Humanity* (Gabriola, BC, Canada: New Society Publishers, 2022).

4. United Nations, "Outcome of the first global stocktake," Conference of the Parties serving as the meeting of the Parties to the Paris Agreement, FCCC/PA/CMA/2023/L.17, 5, 2023. See https://unfccc.int/sites/default/files/resource/cma2023_L17_adv.pdf (accessed January 4, 2024).

5. In 2011 the German Advisory Council on Global Change (WBGU) demanded a "social contract for a great transformation" to determine the transformation towards a regenerative economy and way of life.

6. Karl Polanyi's concept is being used in the present context. See Karl Polanyi, *The Great Transformation. The Political and Economic Origins of our Time* (New York: Farrar & Rinehart, 1944).

7. Dixson-Declève et al., *Earth for All*.

8. This concept, which is widely used today in the German-speaking world, was coined by Egon Becker. See Egon Becker, "Sozial-ökologische Transformation: Anmerkungen zur politischen Ökologie der Nachhaltigkeit" in *Entwicklung und Zusammenarbeit*, vol. 38, issue 1 (1997), pp. 8–11.

9. This way of thinking about the dynamics of equilibrium states, which is now widely accepted, originally goes back to Hermann Haken's work on principles of self-organization. As an introduction, see Hermann Haken, *Erfolgsgeheimnisse der Natur. Synergetik: Die Lehre vom Zusammenwirken* (Reinbek: Rowohlt, 1981).

10. Johan Rockström et al., "Planetary Boundaries: Exploring the Safe Operating Space for Humanity" in *Ecology and Society* vol. 19, issue 2 (2009).

11. McKinsey, "Transformation" in *McKinsey Quarterly*, issue 4, (2019).

12. Kate Raworth, *Doughnut Economics: Seven Ways to Think Like a 21st-Century Economist* (New York: Random House Business, 2017).

13. Timo Meynhardt, "Leadership in the Anthropocene: Recognizing and Counteracting Inequalities in Relation to the Natural World" in Corinne Michaela Flick (ed.), *Equality in an Unequal World* (Munich: Convoco! Editions, 2023), pp. 247–71.

14. Caroline Hickman, Elizabeth Marks, et al., "Climate anxiety in children and young people and their beliefs about government responses to climate change: a global survey" in *The Lancet Planetary Health* vol. 5, issue 12, (2021), e863-e873.

15. Nikolaj Schultz, *Land Sickness* (Cambridge: Polity, 2023).

16. Schultz, *Land Sickness*, p.7.

17. Schultz, *Land Sickness*, p. 4.

18. Schultz, *Land Sickness*, p. 67.

19. Meynhardt et al., *Führen in der Krise*.

20. Ibid.

CHAPTER 13

RELATIONS, NETWORKS, AND ENTANGLEMENTS: THE ANTHROPOCENE AS A CHALLENGE TO MODERN DEMOCRATIC GOVERNANCE IN EUROPE

CLAUDIA WIESNER

INTRODUCTION

The concept of the Anthropocene is relatively recent. Coined in 2000 in the natural and earth sciences,[1] the concept is today used in different ways. On the one hand, the Anthropocene names a new geological era, signaling that after the era of the Holocene Earth has, for about 70 years now, been in the Anthropocene, a period where human-induced changes are marking the planet decisively. Visibly humans have by now had such a great impact on nature that they are decisively affected by it in return. The planetary ecological and geological system is becoming increasingly unstable and vulnerable, and this directly affects humans and their lives. Backfire effects such as climate change underline the fact that humans themselves are part of nature. On the other hand, the Anthropocene brings a challenge to modern thinking and ontology. Two core ideas of modern thinking are questioned in particular: the idea of a separation between humans/culture and nature, as mentioned above, and the idea of linearity and simple causality in human action and in politics. Instead, we have to face the fact that all life on the planet functions in complex systems and entanglements that models of causality and linearity fail to grasp. In sum, the Anthropocene refers to a changing global, human, and natural condition that challenges modern conceptions of both knowledge and agency.[2] This chapter discusses the challenges that the Anthropocene—understood both as a new geological epoch and a questioning of the modern episteme—poses for democratic governance in Europe, both in theory and practice.

THE ANTHROPOCENE AND DEMOCRACY

The Anthropocene thus marks an inevitable turning point, both for modernist thinking and modern modes of governance. Modernity seemed to have succeeded in making the world readable and thus governable based on linearity, causality, and progress. Like the socialist version of modernity more than 30 years ago, this world view has now been challenged. The Anthropocene entails the end of the stable geological epoch of the Holocene that has made possible the modern illusion of a stable stage and linear progress for human history. It seems that the modern order is deteriorating in a material, but non-linear way. The future no longer appears as a promise of progress. This triggers feelings of vulnerability, precariousness, and uncertainty. The Anthropocene is thus often linked to imaginaries of decay, loss of control, and apocalypse[3] that no longer concern only the peripheries but also the centers of global capitalism and liberal democracy.[4] Moreover, in the Anthropocene, established modes of governance and democracy no longer work "as they used too" or "as they should." Governance is no longer simple or a matter of rational control and regulation; it does not follow linear causality schemes (if it ever did). In sum, the complex and entangled problems of the

Anthropocene cannot be governed using simple and linear modes of governance.

The Anthropocene's ontological insecurity, i.e., the crisis of modern thinking and knowledge, the insecurities this entails, and the incapacity to govern effectively, at least in certain areas and fields, fuels the series of "crises" of modern democratic governance we currently experience, and their symptoms such as populism and technocracy. Outside the Anthropocene debate, these crisis symptoms are generally discussed as part of a general "crisis of democracy."[5] When seen in relation to the condition of the Anthropocene, the picture becomes much broader: the crisis of democracy is then directly linked to and embedded in the challenges posed by the Anthropocene and the broader crisis of modernity and modern modes of thinking, governance, and democracy.[6]

Given this diagnosis, how can, how should, democratic governance in both theory and practice react to the Anthropocene, especially in the face of the current symptoms of democracy in crisis? In their search for alternative theories and concepts for thinking and governing in the Anthropocene, academic debate as well as political strategies in the last decade have increasingly turned towards concepts such as complexity, resilience, quantum theories, adaptation, entanglements, materialisms, and relationality. This discussion then involves conceptions, possibilities, and practices that hold the potential to translate democracy into an entangled world.[7]

Regarding governmental practice, governing democratically in the Anthropocene means to govern complexity, because, given the challenges described, government must take into account the entanglements of the Anthropocene rather than governing simple and clearly separated policy fields. As a concrete example, "climate change" does not describe a policy field like, for example, education policy, but a related set of symptoms and problems that are linked and that cut across from environmental via economic and social to migration and foreign policy. In order to tackle climate change or other Anthropocene challenges, democratic governance therefore needs to rely on a more systemic approach, think in networks, and take into account that there is no effect of a policy or action that does not also have a side-effect. This thinking is at odds with a policy field tradition that is used to separating fields, with, for example, healthcare, nature protection, and economics being separate portfolios. While it is thus already difficult to govern Anthropocene complexity, it is even more complicated to do this democratically.

GOVERNING THE ANTHROPOCENE IN EUROPE

How are the challenges of the Anthropocene taken up currently in Europe, both conceptually and in practice? In brief, so far they are not necessarily taken up as new, complex, and entangled Anthropocene problem constellations. Issues such as climate change, security, new technologies, or artificial intelligence are rather still discussed and treated in terms of a policy field logic.

The EU is a case in point of such an approach. As an EU scholar it is easy to notice a double gap in this respect. First, the EU is heavily engaged in issues such as climate change, security, new technologies, or artificial intelligence, but so far, these fields are not discussed in connection to the Anthropocene debates and approaches, nor do EU policy documents highlight the Anthropocene as a concept. Second, while the Anthropocene as a challenge is debated in International Relations and Political Theory alike, this is not yet the case for the academic debates on Europe and the European Union. So why does the EU as a polity tackle Anthropocene problems, but, as it seems, not in an Anthropocene way? And why is the academic debate on the EU not addressing the question?

According to many accounts in the Anthropocene academic debate, "Eurocentric thinking" might be the reason. It is assumed that Eurocentrism can be equated with all the downsides of modernity such as colonialism, rationalist and bureaucratic thinking, the destruction of nature, and oppression of the Global South.[8] However, such accounts come mostly without giving a definition of what Eurocentrism actually means. Moreover, the "Europe" they refer to is nonexistent. Europe has not one, but various contested meanings, intellectual traditions, or values.[9] To assume there is one Europe that incorporates a clearly defined set of ideas which in addition represent the dark sides of Enlightenment is, in short, an essentializing simplification. Moreover, it needs to be highlighted that Europe and the sets of ideas and traditions as well as political practices it stands for is not identical to the European Union.[10] This also means that it is too simple to claim that the EU does react in a technocratic way to the Anthropocene challenges because it is an outcome of the downsides of Enlightenment. The picture is more complex, and the path to it is more winding.

THE EU, DEMOCRACY, AND EXPERTISE

The EU as a polity has its roots in the idea of overcoming two outcomes of earlier modernist thinking: namely, nation states and wars. The idea of European unification is an old utopia that over the course of centuries has been associated with high-aiming normative goals such as a more peaceful and democratic Europe. The European unification process, however, was not linear and straightforward but marked by manifold controversies regarding the character of the polity that was in the making. To better understand the EU's different rationales, it is useful to take a closer look at the conceptual controversies at the basis of European unification.[11]

One core conceptual controversy is the conflict between two possible goals of unification: a "realist" balance-of-power conception, aimed at sovereign nation states; and a democratic European federation, attributing a key role to EU citizens, being democratically governed, and aimed at reducing or abandoning the role of the nation states. The balance-of-power conception of a united Europe was coined and put forward by the movement of the "European Unionists." They aimed to safeguard peace in Europe and create a unified Europe, but they wanted it to consist of sovereign nation states, which should be coordinated by a European Council.[12] On the other hand, the movements of the "European Federalists" believed that a democratic European federation that transcended the nation states was the only way to make Europe progress in peace and freedom.[13] The guiding principles of this federation should be democracy, civil liberties and rights, pluralism, and decentralization. Europe in that context should be neutral and choose a third way between a capitalist economy and a planned economy.[14] While the Unionists were thus clearly anchored in modern linear thinking, oriented at nation states and linear progress, the Federalists were already thinking in complexities, networks, and relationalities.

The Federalists were mostly activists and resistance fighters and had the main role in pushing forward European integration between 1940 and 1945. The Unionists, represented in the United Europe Movement (UEM) founded in 1947, mobilized leaders in politics, the economy, and the media for their ideas: for example, the new leaders of the European nation states such as Adenauer and de Gaulle.[15] Starting with the Congress of the Hague in 1948,[16] the European integration process became largely based on nation states and their governments along with their modern rationalities, rather than on European citizens and entanglements.[17] But until today the EU is marked by the key controversy between a balance-of-power Europe and a democratic Europe.[18]

Another key conceptual controversy in the EU is the one between democracy and expertise. When European unification was finally initiated after World War II, it was not only led by a relatively small and elitist group. Expertise, bureaucracy, and technocracy became characteristics of EU decision-making.[19] Expertise has been one of the founding principles of the EU Commission. The French system of recruiting the best-qualified candidates for the EU bureaucracy has helped give it a strongly expert-based and technocratic character. The founding figures Jean Monnet and Robert Schuman, moreover, were both suspicious of representative democracy and elected officials, because they wanted "to shield Europe from the passion, folly, and fluctuations of political will."[20]

The European Union thus not only incorporates and practices a rationalist modern ideal of governing, it is also expert-oriented. The expert-oriented model of governance has been applied in the EU whenever crisis symptoms became visible, or when it was difficult to tackle problems in the institutional triangle of Commission, Council, and Parliament. Hence the EU has instituted a number of agencies over the decades that tackle key political problems, mostly with thin democratic legitimation and a pronounced role of experts.[21]

THE EU'S APPROACH TO THE ANTHROPOCENTRIC CHALLENGES

I will now briefly discuss how crucial Anthropocene problems such as climate change, artificial intelligence, and security are taken up and governed by the European Union, asking which strategies and patterns of governance are deployed and how they refer (or not) to governing complexity, networks, and systems.

One example is the key action on climate change, the Green Deal.[22] It is crucially linked to an increase in regulatory mechanisms, mainly by a taxonomy that aims to take note of all kinds of cost–benefit and damage analyses with regard to climate, but also social policy. This taxonomy aims to tackle complexity by controlling and regulating it. Governing the challenges of climate change is taken up by the EU as the challenge to govern more complexity, and the solution means more regulation and control. This also means governance that is more bureaucratic and less democratic.

In the EU's papers on resilience, strategic autonomy, etc., a similar pattern is visible. There is a bulk of crisis response mechanisms and white papers, there are resilience reports, resilience dashboards, and resilience marker general guidelines.[23] The papers quite hopefully line up expert-based approaches on how to counter the strategic challenges of creating a resilient, strategically autonomous EU in a changing global order and in the face of natural disasters. The idea that is clearly shining through is, again, that more complexity just requires better, more complex, and more expert-based governance mechanisms—in other words, more of the same.

The EU, in sum, largely reacts to the Anthropocene in the modern, rationalist, linear, and expertise-oriented way of governing it has been developing and practicing over decades. The Anthropocene challenges of climate change, security, new technologies, or artificial intelligence are dealt with as complex policy fields, bringing more complexity than ever before that accordingly require more complex and more expert-based mechanisms of governance, more technocracy, more control, more bureaucracy, and hence also more depoliticization and less democracy.

First, this way of reacting proceeds, as is often the case with the EU, sometimes at the expense of thick modes of legitimation – but not always, as many of the respective policy measures and packages are decided upon jointly by the European Parliament and the Council. However, all in all, expert-based and bureaucratic ways of governing the Anthropocene strengthen the problems the EU already shows in terms of democratic decision-making.[24] To rely on expert-based modes of governance often means reducing the impact of democratically legitimized fora of deliberation and decision-making, and it means reducing public debate and transparency, because experts usually discuss behind closed doors. To increase bureaucracy also means increasing the workloads of people who have to deal with the new bureaucratic requirements, and it means enhancing citizens' sense of a distant bureaucratic and technocratic world populated by "those above." These tendencies not only already exist in the EU, they are also already perceived as problems,[25] which means that to intensify them will most probably intensify criticism too.

As an important side note in this context, the arguments of pro-climate NGOs such as Fridays for Future are not that dissimilar from those of the EU institutions, since they claim to give experts a stronger say in governing climate change than representative democratic institutions. In this, their criticism of representative democracy can be harsher and more pronounced than that of the EU's institutions—EU institutions would not openly criticize representative democracy.

Second, the overview of the EU's responses to Anthropocene challenges indicates that instead of governing Anthropocene complexity with complexity-oriented tools and approaches, complexity is divided into separate clusters or even policy fields and controlled by expertise and bureaucracy. This means that the EU's approaches still try to control things in classical ways and do not tackle the needs specific to the Anthropocene. The EU does not react to the challenge posed to the modern episteme and to the visible limits of cause-and-effect-related thinking by questioning them, but by applying them even more fervently in its aims to govern Anthropocene challenges. A key question then is to what extent such a kind of policy-field and expertise-based reaction has a chance to succeed. Can the complex problems set by the Anthropocene be tackled by more complex, more expert-oriented technocratic and more bureaucratic answers at all? This is at least doubtful. The EU's reaction mechanisms will probably encounter limits, since more chaos cannot be countered by more control.

As said above, governing the Anthropocene must take into account various entanglements, rely on systemic approaches, think in networks, and accept that there is no effect of a policy or action that does not also have a side-effect. Instead of the EU's policy field orientation, bureaucracy, and technocracy, what is needed is more complexity-oriented approaches, such as, for example, quantum-theoretical and chaos-theoretical ones.[26] Complex governance must embrace complexity, it means embracing the fact that there is no simple cause-and-effect relation, and no action without unintended effects. This includes the realization that we cannot fully know what the cascade of effects of an action will be. All of politics is contingent. Every political action must be based on this idea, which means that complex problem settings should be tackled as such and take account of the full picture, rather than being split into policy fields again. Of course, in this, expert opinions can indicate successful ways of treating complex problems such as climate change, but experts cannot deliver simple recipes for solving the problem. In order to enable democratic governance in the Anthropocene, the goal would thus be to embrace complexity and relationality, to search for networked solutions, to think in entanglements, and to abandon the search for linear causalities.

Notes

1   Paul J. Crutzen and Eugene F. Stoermer, "The 'Anthropocene' (2000)" in *The Future of Nature: Documents of Global Change*, eds. Libby Robin, Sverker Sörlin, and Paul Warde (New Haven: Yale University Press, 2013), pp. 479–90.

2   For a detailed discussion of the various facets of the Anthropocene see e.g. David Chandler, Franziska Müller, and Delf Rothe (eds.), *International Relations in the Anthropocene* (London: Palgrave Macmillan, 2021).

3   See e.g. Anna Lowenhaupt Tsing, *The Mushroom at the End of the World: On the Possibility of Life in Capitalist Ruins* (Princeton/Oxford: Princeton University Press, 2021).

4   Bruno Latour, *Down to Earth: Politics in the New Climatic Regime* (Cambridge: Polity Press, 2018).

5   Claudia Wiesner, "Democratic Equality and Changes in Modern Liberal Democracies" in *Equality in an Unequal World*, ed. Corinne M. Flick, (Munich: Convoco Editions, 2023).

6   Latour, *Down to Earth*.

7   Aysem Mert, "Challenges to Democracy in the Anthropocene" in Chandler et al., *International Relations in the Anthropocene*, pp. 291–309.

8   Cheryl Mc Ewan, "Decolonising the Anthropocene" in Chandler et al., *International Relations in the Anthropocene*.

9   Claudia Wiesner and Meike Schmidt-Gleim (eds.), *The Meanings of Europe* (London: Routledge, 2014).

10 Ibid., pp. 1–18.

11 Claudia Wiesner, *Inventing the EU as a Democratic Polity: Concepts, Actors and Controversies* (London: Palgrave Macmillan, 2019).

12 Frank Niess, *Die Europäische Idee – Aus dem Geist des Widerstands* (Frankfurt am Main: Suhrkamp, 2001), pp. 126–30.

13 See in detail Walter Lipgens, *The Struggle for European Union by Political Parties and Pressure Groups in Western European Countries 1945–1950 (Including 252 Documents in Their Orig. Language on 6 Microfiches)* (Berlin: de Gruyter, 1988), pp. 545–49.

14 See, for example, Altiero Spinelli and Ernesto Rossi, "The Ventotene Manifesto," 1944, http://www.altierospinelli.org/manifesto/en/pdf/manifesto1944en.pdf (accessed November 13, 2023).

15 Niess, *Die Europäische Idee*, pp. 126–51; Curt Gasteyger, *Europa zwischen Spaltung und Einigung 1945 bis 1993: Darstellung und Dokumentation* (Bonn: Bundeszentrale für Politische Bildung, 1994), pp. 25–32.

16 Niess, *Die Europäische Idee*, pp. 164–73.

17 European Movement, 2013. "EMI History. The Congress of the Hague. Resolutions," http://www.europeanmovement.eu/index.php?id=6788#c20680 (accessed November 13, 2023).

18 See in detail Wiesner, *Inventing the EU as a Democratic Polity*.

19 On the following, see in detail Cecile Robert, "Depoliticization at the European Level. Delegitimization and Circumvention of Representative Democracy" in *Rethinking Politicisation in Politics, Sociology and International Relations*, ed. Claudia Wiesner (London: Palgrave Macmillan, 2021).

20 Ibid., p. 212.

21 Claudia Wiesner, "Representative Democracy in Financial Crisis Governance: New Challenges in the EU Multilevel System" in *Executive-Legislative (Im)balance in the European*

Union, eds. Diane Fromage, Anna Herranz-Sualles, and Thomas Christiansen (Oxford: Hart Publishing, 2021).

22 European Commission, "A European Green Deal," 2023, https://commission.europa.eu/strategy-and-policy/priorities-2019-2024/european-green-deal_en (accessed November 13, 2023).

23 See e.g. European Council. "How the EU Responds to Crises and Builds Resilience," 2023, https://www.consilium.europa.eu/en/policies/eu-crisis-response-resilience/ (accessed November 13, 2023); European Commission, "Recovery and Resilience Facility," 2023, https://commission.europa.eu/business-economy-euro/economic-recovery/recovery-and-resilience-facility_en (accessed November 13, 2023).

24 Wiesner, *Inventing the EU as a Democratic Polity*, pp. 281–301; Wiesner, "Representative Democracy in Financial Crisis Governance."

25 In my Jean Monnet Chair project "Bridging the Gap" (https://www.hs-fulda.de/forschen/forschungseinrichtungen/wissenschaftliche-zentren-und-forschungsverbuende/cinteus/standard-titel-2) and in the research project "Debating Europe" (www.debating-europe.de) we carry out focus group discussions with Masters students in EU studies in Bulgaria, Croatia, Finland, France, Germany, and Slovenia. A key finding is that the students experience the EU as untransparent, elitist, and distant from its citizens.

26 James Der Derian and Alexander Wendt, *Quantum International Relations* (Oxford: Oxford University Press, 2022).

CHAPTER 14

THE INTERNATIONAL TRADING SYSTEM IN TURMOIL: FROM A POSITIVE-SUM GAME TO A ZERO-SUM GAME—AND BACK AGAIN?

GABRIEL FELBERMAYR

ON ABSOLUTE AND RELATIVE TRADE GAINS

The international trade system and its institutions are in turmoil. After the end of the Cold War and especially with the founding of the World Trade Organization (WTO), the system was characterized by the logic of a positive-sum game. The core of this logic is that all countries participating in the international division of labor benefit from it at the same time and therefore it is a relatively liberal system operating in everyone's interests. However, for various reasons this logic has lost its power of persuasion. International trade is once again increasingly seen as a zero-sum or even negative-sum game. In this model, participation in a liberal international trade system always generates countries that lose, and their loss is seen as a condition of the winners' gains. It is sometimes even claimed that the losses of the losers exceed the gains of those that profit.

This philosophy contradicts the simple theory of comparative advantage that has been taught in lectures at economics departments since David Ricardo.[1] This theory, which can certainly be extended to real-life situations in lots of different economic sectors, complex supply networks, and many countries,[2] emphasizes the existence of absolute trade gains. But it also allows for countries to benefit from world trade to different extents. Typically, trade liberalization leads to poorer or smaller countries initially catching up in relative terms, because the more the situation in individual countries differs from conditions on the world markets, the greater the absolute trade gains. It is therefore easily possible that all countries benefit from free trade in absolute terms, but to relatively different extents. In this case the international division of labor does not of course generate absolute losers, but it does create relative losers. In the context of current politics, we can say that China's admission into the World Trade Organization in 2001 has increased the absolute level of prosperity of many countries but has reduced the relative advantage of industrialized countries' level of prosperity over China as an emerging country.

Why do such trade policy conflicts keep occurring, increasingly so over the last 15 years? Political science has long distinguished between absolute and relative trade gains.[3] In trade wars, typically the absolute level of prosperity of all those involved declines (theoretically there can also be absolute gains under very specific circumstances). But if the reciprocal introduction of trade barriers causes greater damage in one country than in the other, then the result is a relative shift in economic weight to the disadvantage of one country and to the advantage of the other. The issue is how, in politicians' objectives, absolute and relative trade gains are weighted (a positive question) or should be weighted (a normative question). The liberal position focuses on absolute gains, positive-sum logic, and cooperation; the realistic position on relative gains, zero- or even negative-sum logic, and conflict. Part of the drama is that in a positive-sum game all key players must be willing to cooperate; if just one major country opts out, then cooperation no longer provides an equilibrium.[4] The question now arises as to what causes the relative importance of positive-sum logic versus zero-sum logic in international politics?

THE TEMPTATION OF PROTECTIONISM

The simplest theoretical constructs looking at the impact of the international division of labor on prosperity compare situations with and without trade. Now, we can undoubtedly object that this static theoretical perspective is too simplistic. When the technical capabilities of countries change, this affects their trading partners. For example, if China makes technological advances so that productivity increases in the sector for which it previously imported from the rest of the world, then this allows China to improve its position in relation to its partner countries. In addition to the pure productivity effect, China increases its economic output, because increased Chinese production means that imported goods become cheaper on the world market relative to export goods.[5] At the same time and mirroring this, the comparative advantage of China's trading partners and with it their real economic output (real gross domestic product [GDP]) diminishes.[6] The condition for this is that a country is sufficiently large to be able to exert influence on the global market. This is certainly the case for China, the US, and the EU. In the case of individual sectors or goods, even small countries can have large world market shares, so their policies can influence prices on the global markets.[7]

Because one country's export goods must necessarily be other countries' import goods, a change in relative prices on the world markets always creates winners and losers. They are therefore in themselves an expression of a zero-sum game. If technological improvements abroad make Europe's or the US's export goods cheaper relative to their import goods, then this is economically damaging for Europe or the US, regardless of why the export goods have become relatively cheaper. If technological improvements in a country's import sector affect exchange relationships, then this nevertheless has the effect of increasing global production and global prosperity, even if the country's export partners to date lose out. Furthermore, it is still better for trading partners to remain open to trade than to close themselves off, because the level of prosperity achieved through self-sufficiency is lower than that reached through trade, even if the gains from trade may reduce. Furthermore, technological progress in China's export sector is an advantage for its trading partners because their imports become cheaper relative to their exports. The empirical question then arises as to whether China's technological progress over recent decades can be attributed more to the import or to the export sector. Research shows that it could be seen in all sectors, thus making it beneficial to China's trading partners too.[8]

There are also lots of economic policy options that countries can use to try to reduce the relative prices of imported goods on the world market. The classic way is for a country to impose wisely chosen import tariffs.[9] Of course this makes prices more expensive for domestic consumers, but because the demand for imported goods decreases as a result, the (pre-tariff) prices for these goods on the world market fall. This improves the position of the country imposing the tariffs, but damages trading partners. This is where the character of such a measure becomes apparent: it creates winners and losers. As a rule, the losers lose more than the winners win—it is a negative-sum game. The situation is further exacerbated if the country affected responds with its own import tariffs. Then all countries involved lose out.

Prices for imported goods on the world markets can also be manipulated using other instruments, such as subsidizing production costs. This also harms the exporting country, but the economic effects in the importing country are less clear because the subsidies have to be paid for. Theoretically, gains can also be achieved for individual countries by manipulating world market prices for export goods, for example through well-chosen taxation of exports, which can lead to an increase in prices of export goods on the world market. In this way, the exporting country improves its position at the expense of its trading partners, even if its exports decline as a result. Export restrictions have similarly damaging effects on trading partners. However, they do not create government revenue, instead directly increasing the profits of the export sector. Nevertheless, as a rule, such measures always reduce global prosperity, and if the country affected responds with reciprocal measures, then there are only absolute losers.

TRUST AS THE CONDITION FOR POSITIVE-SUM GAMES

A central condition for realizing positive-sum gains is the existence of enough trust that trading partners do not opportunistically exploit dependencies arising from the specialization that is logically inherent to the international division of labor, or that unequal (but positive!) trade gains arising from the country that benefits relatively more are not used in terms of power politics against its trading partner. If this trust does not exist, then the international division of labor seems risky. Interestingly, this problem has been well known since the early days of modern economic theory. In his great work *The Wealth of Nations* (1776), Adam Smith highlighted the advantages of the division of labor on the one hand, while on the other hand also warning that one-sided dependencies could threaten England's security. For this reason, he praised the so-called "Navigation Act" that banned Dutch ships from loading and unloading in English ports as "maybe the wisest of all the commercial regulations of England." For Smith there was a clear hierarchy: the security of the country was more important to him than material prosperity ("defence, however, is of much more importance than opulence").[10]

So the fact that the international division of labor can create dependencies that can be abused for geopolitical reasons is not a new insight. The General Agreement on Tariffs and Trade (GATT), the central pillar of our international trade system, includes in Article 21 a so-called national security exemption, which allows countries to withdraw their obligations with respect to the WTO if they are threatened in terms of security policy. This means that countries can introduce tariffs, even though this was actually ruled out in the negotiations that led to WTO accession. This reflects considerations that can also be found in Adam Smith's work. Donald Trump invoked this very Article 21 of GATT when he imposed aluminum and steel tariffs in 2018 due to a perceived threat to American security.

In the past, the leap from trade wars to military conflicts was not uncommon, so it makes perfect sense that postwar trade policy sought to prevent such scenarios. However, the institutional framework created to do this required a sufficient level of trust between countries, because the enforcement of such rules through international law is subject to tight limits.

THE WORLD TRADE ORGANIZATION AND ITS CRISIS

The General Agreement on Tariffs and Trade (GATT), which was adopted in 1947 and which, in early 1995, gave rise to a multilateral institution, the WTO, was initially negotiated by just 18 members—all victorious powers in World War II, allies of the US, or

British colonies on the way to independence. Western European countries joined gradually—for example, Germany and Austria in 1951; Japan joined in 1955. Initially there was little disagreement between these countries regarding the need for cooperation. The US was clearly hegemonic. This created trust in the compliance of the countries involved. Over the years, more and more countries have joined GATT. The systemic rival Soviet Union has never been a member of GATT, although some Warsaw Pact countries such as Poland and Romania signed the agreement in the 1960s. China ratified the text only in 1986, despite being a founding party. By the time of the fall of the Berlin Wall, GATT had been ratified by 95 countries. This means that the system by no means encompassed all countries in the world; it was multilateral because a large number of member states mutually agreed on tariff reductions and legally binding rules, but it was neither global nor omnilateral. It was, rather, a club of relatively like-minded countries with the US as the undisputed pacesetter. The aspiration to be truly global only came about after the collapse of the Soviet Union. While two countries on average joined GATT every year in the first 40 years of its existence, between 1990 and 1994 33 states joined in just five years, including heavyweights such as Saudi Arabia.

GATT is a framework that has regulated world trade, but not yet a world trade system. It was only the founding of the WTO in 1995 that saw the emergence of a truly global framework and an institution. It has various elements, for example the most-favored nation clause (Article 1 of GATT, which was, so to speak, institutionalized in the WTO). This says that if a country wants to give an advantage to one trading partner, for example through a low tariff, then it must grant this low tariff to all trading partners. This reflects the anti-bloc formation doctrine of the international trading system. In addition, reciprocity is also required in negotiations. This has been the operating mode of GATT and WTO for decades and a kind of safety valve for damage control if something "bad" happens. Although punitive tariffs are often talked about, in essence penalties do not exist. If a rule violation takes place, the extent of the economic damage is determined, and this can then be compensated for through appropriate measures, such as countervailing duties. The fact that this is not a punishment is important, because these rules show that considerations arising from power politics cause a breakdown in the principles of GATT and the WTO.

In any event, on January 1, 1995, after years of negotiations, the WTO was finally founded. In addition to

GATT, the contractual basis for this also includes a General Agreement on Trade in Services (GATS) and the *Agreement on Trade*-Related Aspects of Intellectual Property Rights (TRIPS). The WTO has a secretariat that has hardly any right of initiative of its own. However, there is a two-tier dispute resolution body and an administrative body that is primarily intended to ensure transparency about trading conditions. All GATT signatory states joined the WTO when it was founded; 36 other countries quickly followed. China joined in November 2001, and Russia in August 2012. The most recent accession was Afghanistan in July 2016; there have been no accessions since then. In addition to the 164 members, there are 25 observer states that are officially in accession negotiations (often over a period of decades), such as Iran, Iraq, Serbia, Belarus, and Ethiopia.

In recent years the international trading system has run into crisis. One main cause of this was the economic and financial crisis of 2008/09 which fundamentally undermined confidence in the global market economy and its institutions. While the countries of the West, especially the US and the EU, went into major recessions with high unemployment and the rescue of the banking systems required massive government bailouts, China has remained on the path of growth.

The narrative of a liberal world economy that enables absolute gains for all or at least most countries lost a great deal of credibility. In addition, the impact of the expansion of WTO membership and the integration of emerging countries, primarily China, into the global economy became clear: these countries have benefited more relatively speaking than their Western trading partners. Their economic convergence made them stronger in terms of political power, so that they were suddenly perceived as systemic rivals. Their new self-confidence also emerged following the invention of the BRICS group of countries in 2003 by the investment bank Goldman Sachs. This was initially about marketing for a fund, but it led to an official affiliation between Brazil, Russia, India, China and, somewhat later, South Africa, as an alternative to the West's economic and political model.

Another key challenge is that the system has lost its undisputed hegemon, the US, which is withdrawing partly of its own accord and is in part simply losing influence due to the rise of the emerging economies.

As a result of this loss of confidence, many governments' objectives began to focus less on absolute trade gains and more on relative trade gains. Achieving absolute welfare benefits took a back seat to maintaining or expanding a margin of safety from systemic rivals. A willingness to cooperate gave way to the conviction that they had to arm themselves against opportunistic attacks from other countries. Protectionist measures of all kinds increased and initiatives to promote trade liberalization became rarer.

FROM HYPERGLOBALIZATION TO SLOWBALIZATION

The consequences of this rethink are shown very clearly in Figure 1. While global trade in goods and services grew significantly faster than GDP after the mid-1980s, this trend came to an end in 2008. Since then, trade has been very volatile. More importantly, trade in goods tends to grow more slowly than GDP; trade in services at about the same speed. It is precisely in goods trade that countries' protectionist measures, for example in the form of tariffs, have increased most significantly.

Figure 1 makes it clear: the period of so-called "hyperglobalization" (1988–2008) is over.[11] It didn't last long; less than twenty years. So historically it was a relatively short phase, an historical anomaly, during which there really existed *one* global economy, a shared conviction in the beneficial effects of global integration, and a profound political will to cooperate. The new era is one of sideways movement, of "slowbalization."[12]

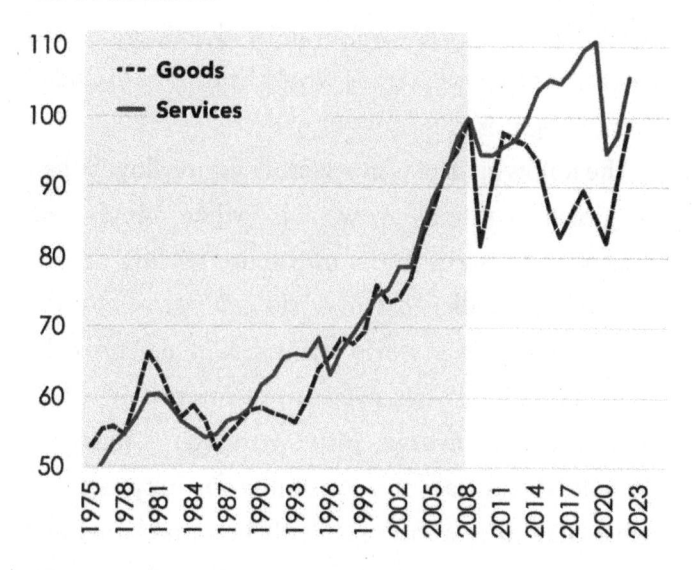

Fig. 1 *World Trade in Relation to Global GDP, Index 2008=100*[13]

Researchers are investigating the extent to which increased protectionism can actually be blamed for the end of hyperglobalization. To do this, it is important to understand what drives the growth of trade. First of all, some of it is down to methodological artifacts. Thirty years ago, when Prague and Bratislava traded with each other, this did not appear in any trade statistics. But now the cities are in two different countries, the Czech Republic and Slovakia, and so we suddenly have more trade. The former Czechoslovakia is just one example of many where countries have split. Of course, that's not what we mean by globalization and, strictly speaking, such trade would have to be excluded from the figures.

The following fact is much more interesting. When the global economy grows, i.e., when supply and demand increase in the world, more trading occurs. Our models predict that if world GDP grows by 1%, then, *ceteris paribus*, world trade should also grow by about 1%. Things get even more interesting when country sizes converge. Fifty years ago, China, for example, could claim responsibility for only 2–3% of global GDP. If a country suddenly becomes larger and more relevant as a trading partner, this will also drive up the total global trade flows. A more equally distributed global landscape of gross domestic products also encourages trade.

The above discussion raises the question of what impact trade policy measures have. Tariffs are central to trade policy; they are typically the subject of negotiations or pillars of a protectionist policy. From an empirical perspective, however, non-tariff barriers, especially regulatory measures, are more important for driving changes in world trade. The latest research also clearly shows that, in addition to tariff levels and regulatory agreements, uncertainties are often important.[14] For example, the uncertainty about what tariffs European automobile exporters to the US will face over the next few years has led to a massive redesign of business models, even though the US has (so far) refrained from introducing such import barriers (which go against WTO regulations). It's unsurprising because, after all, investments are always necessary, for example in the network of dealerships, etc., and uncertainty makes such investments uninteresting. In such a case it is better to produce locally for the local market. The question of how to deal with political uncertainty is therefore a very important one.

Another question that is heavily debated by researchers is whether trade, as depicted in Figure 1, and other forms of globalization—for example the mobility of capital, people, or knowledge across borders—are complements or substitutes. Empirical research clearly concludes that these are complements. If the international mobility of people is restricted or banned in a sanctions regime, this always affects trade. On the other hand, if people are allowed to move freely, typically this drives up trade flows as well.

Lastly—and of profound empirical importance—technological progress is also important for the size of trade flows relative to gross domestic product—consider, for example, the steamships of the 19th and early 20th centuries, the railways, containerization during the last century, and the information technologies of today.

There are studies that attempt to compare these different drivers of global trade. Overall, it can be said that in the long term it is technological changes that are driving the world's openness the most. Political cycles can be identified around this long-term trend. There have been repeated episodes in which tariffs have been lowered, followed by a backlash against globalization. This story goes back to the 19th century. Today we are probably in a situation where the widespread loss of confidence and the resulting serious political uncertainty are slowing down globalization. But the underlying technological trend continues, because technical progress can almost never be halted or even reversed politically.

Nevertheless, it is undisputed that the world has become more protectionist. However, it is not easy to measure this increase correctly, because it is not tariffs that have increased particularly, but rather a variety of regulatory, non-tariff measures. A team at the University of St. Gallen is attempting to examine laws passed around the world to see whether they have discriminatory elements, i.e., whether they have led to overseas suppliers being discriminated against by comparison with domestic suppliers. If that is the case, we can say that these are trade barriers. The individual measures are added up—although this is a case of "comparing apples with oranges", the resulting measure is still meaningful (Fig. 2). It shows how over the last 15 years, since 2009, the number of new restrictive measures introduced annually has increased. There have also been liberalizing policies, but their number has been significantly lower each year than the number of restrictive policies.

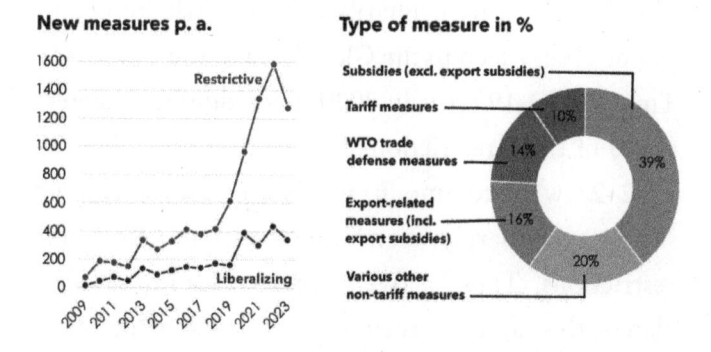

Fig. 2 *Discriminating Trade Policy Measures Worldwide*[15]

What discriminatory measures are now being used? In the main they are subsidies. In addition, these include the above-mentioned non-tariff measures, as well as export-related measures (both subsidies and restrictions), and measures that the WTO allows. (The WTO permits countries to impose protective tariffs under certain conditions, for example if a very high amount of imports appear very quickly that can wipe out entire industry sectors, or if another country is engaging in "dumping.")

The classic tariff measures, i.e. those that are implemented in violation of WTO law (for example, if there were a 25% tariff on European cars, as US President Trump threatened), make up the smallest proportion of these discriminatory measures at just 10%.

Among the restrictive measures that have appeared in recent years are primarily export restrictions. This can be clearly seen in the Global Trade Alert database. The COVID-19 crisis in 2020 saw a significant emergence of these restrictions for the first time. Even in 2022–23, when commodity prices, especially in the food sector, rose sharply, many countries imposed export restrictions. These actively hinder exports. At first glance, this does not seem to fit into the mercantilist ideology that many citizens, politicians, and bureaucrats still adhere to, namely that exports are good and imports are bad. But if goods are prevented from going abroad and are kept at home, this will of course lower prices at home and combat inflation. That's why we see such instruments being used especially in periods of inflation. India, for example, restricted the export of rice in July 2023 in order to curb domestic prices. This is a major problem for many countries that depend on importing food from India.

Otherwise, 20% of export-related measures are capital controls. This too is a worrying trend. Capital controls are used to monitor and potentially prohibit certain domestic investments abroad or foreign investments in the domestic market, for example in the case of dual-use technologies.

THE IMPACT OF PROTECTIONISM

Figure 3 shows an index of the openness of the world from a legal perspective. Researchers in the KOF Swiss Economic Institute at ETH Zürich have tried to define the openness of the world *de jure*, i.e. what laws exist to facilitate trade and the mobility of capital, etc., and to condense this information into the form of an index. What is striking is that this *de jure* index of openness and the actual level of openness that we see *de facto* in the markets appear to be correlated. Of course, we should not immediately read a causal connection from a correlation. Perhaps countries have become more open because they could afford to. But here we have at least an indication that the end of hyperglobalization has also come about for trade policy reasons. In addition, many studies show how protectionist measures affect trade flows.

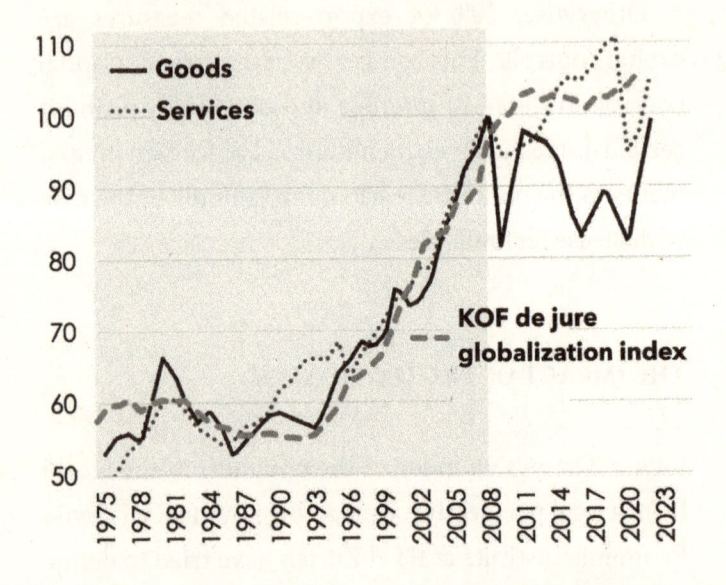

Fig. 3 *The Influence of Political Measures, Index, 2008=100*

It is also clear from figures 1 and 2 that we have not experienced a collapse in global trade, neither in the wake of the COVID-19 crisis nor in the context of the war in Ukraine. World trade has not been growing since 2008, but the graph is moving sideways. This resilience of the international trading system must be taken into account in all the doomsday scenarios that are being debated. What has probably causally driven this development in openness is not so much an increase in protectionism, but primarily the absence of any major new agreements. We have seen little new liberalization of international trade since 2008.

THE RISE OF CHINA

In 2001 China joined the WTO. The accession process had already started a few years earlier (see shaded area in Fig. 4). As a result, many companies went to China in advance in order to trade with China earlier. It was known that joining the WTO would reduce the above-mentioned uncertainty and increase the economic opportunities for cooperation. However, a few years after joining, China stopped opening up further economically, both *de jure* and *de facto*. Around the time of the global economic and financial crisis, China began to withdraw from the global division of labor. *De facto* globalization declined and *de jure* openness moved sideways. Nevertheless, in this phase after the country joined the WTO China has created a tremendous success story, and many observers see a causal connection in this. The fact that China suddenly had access to the global market—not just to consumers in the US and Europe, but especially to Western technologies—triggered this great convergence in China. China's take-off was not really foreseeable in 2001. If the US or Europe had predicted this development, they might have refused China WTO membership or set other, tougher conditions for accession.

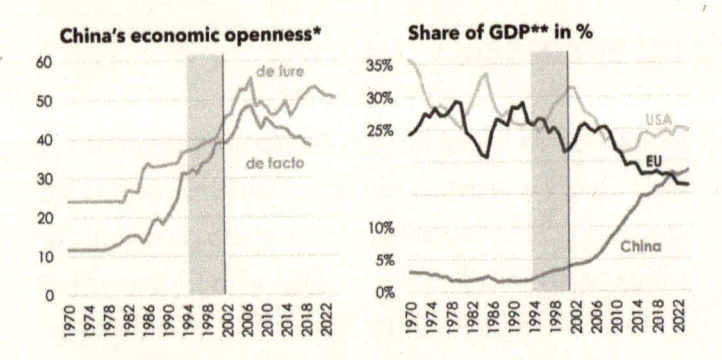

Fig. 4 *The Relative Rise of China*[16]

The rise of China is the West's loss in terms of percentage of world GDP. However, sometimes one may wonder why we are so defeatist. If transatlantic cooperation works and we add the US and Europe together, the situation looks less dire. Nevertheless, significant political resistance has arisen from China's rapid and perhaps surprising convergence, and also because such a strong and rapid opening up of such a large country naturally causes economic damage. There is now a large body of research on "China Syndrome," particularly as it applies to the US, showing that the sharp increase in imports from China has indeed led to deindustrialization, job losses, and increased inequality in many regions of the US. Elsewhere, however, this development has simultaneously led to high profits and lower prices. Overall, I would doubt that this development was bad for the US. What is certain, however, is that it has led to more inequality, especially at the regional level.

OTHER DRIVERS OF GLOBALIZATION SKEPTICISM

In the above, we attributed the increasing skepticism of or opposition to globalization to the fact that China and other emerging countries have gained in importance as a result of this opening up of world markets. This was not intended by the previous dominant global economic powers such as the US or Europe, who enabled China's accession to the WTO in 2001, at least not without a substantial alignment of China's political and economic policies with the Western model. So it can be said that the shift in the global balance of power is certainly a factor.

The second driver of globalization skepticism is increased inequality, not only in the North, but also in middle- and lower-income countries. Jeffry Frieden talks about "compensation failure," i.e., the inability to compensate the losers in globalization.[17] However, I often have the impression that the public ascribes too much weight to the influence of globalization when it is made responsible for undesirable developments at home such as rising inequality. This is a theme that often recurs in economic history, because politically it often seems easier to blame foreigners for grievances. For example, imports are often seen as the cause of the decline of domestic industries, even if there are other reasons for this. I'm not saying that globalization doesn't play a part in the rise of inequality, but domestic conditions are probably quantitatively three to four times more important.

And last, the environmental problem too leads to increased skepticism about globalization. For example, fear of an increase in carbon emissions is an important reason for many activists to oppose the Mercosur trade agreement. There are fears that more trade with South America will mean deforestation of the rainforests. The non-internalization of external effects, for example greenhouse gas emissions, is indeed a serious problem—after all, we have still not managed to put a price on greenhouse gas emissions that are caused by transport, for example, or this is only being done in a very rudimentary way.

The fourth point, which is also being discussed prominently by researchers,[18] is that our global system is still based on nation states with different preferences. The one-size-fits-all idea of an international trading system, in which industrial policy, intellectual property protection, etc. should be the same for all countries, is difficult to reconcile with these differences in national preferences. We can already see in Europe how hard it is to implement a common policy for the internal market because, for example, people in Scandinavia have completely different economic policy views and expectations than in Portugal. This is even more pronounced on a global level. When one-size-fits-all ideas such as the WTO encounter these differences in democratic preferences, resistance to common rules can arise because of a sense of diminished sovereignty in some countries. Countries have the impression that the WTO prohibits them from pursuing their preferences, and even measures allowed by the WTO cannot be implemented as otherwise companies will move away or other things will happen that are too economically damaging. Accordingly, countries abandon their actual preferences and pursue other policies for which there may not be democratic majorities.

All of these factors have led to the erosion of the intellectual, epistemic basis of the global market economy. It no longer has the appeal it had 20 or 30 years ago, when academia, politics, and the public sphere agreed that a global system based on free markets was better because it created prosperity and freedom. This idea has lost some of its power and goes some way to explaining the return to protectionist policies.

A NEW PHASE OF ZERO-SUM LOGIC?

So, are we in a new phase, a phase of zero-sum logic, in geo-economics? I would say that geo-economics is unfortunately not new at all but is actually the natural state of play. We only experienced a different phase between 1990 and 2008. What is interesting is that this debate has so far been carried out primarily by political scientists. For decades, issues of power politics were ignored in economic models, because economists assumed, and often still do, that for governments trade policy means increasing domestic prosperity, that is the absolute level of domestic prosperity. However, for political scientists it is also about relative gains, for which the decisive factor is not only how a trade policy increases a country's own level of prosperity, but also to what extent it increases this level of prosperity relative to possible systemic rivals. As soon as a situation like this occurs, where it's no longer just about absolute prosperity, the models that economists have come up with encounter difficulties. Many of our theorems no longer work, and the economic theory of GATT and WTO is facing problems because externalities suddenly inhibit the validity of classic game-theory results.

In this case, it is no longer important simply how a policy affects a country itself, but also how it affects its neighbors. When these two elements are present, economic logic (a logic of money) and political-science logic (a logic of power), we have a mixture of positive-sum logic and zero-sum logic. Ultimately, only one country can be relatively dominant. When the political science criterion becomes more important, our economic logics often no longer work. In this case, for example, we can no longer show that the rules of WTO and GATT lead to cooperation and we would therefore have to consider these systems differently.

It is a fundamental problem for GATT, WTO, and the other multilateral institutions that governments' objectives have changed. It's no longer just about making yourself better off in absolute terms, but it's also about making systemic rivals relatively small. This perspective also follows Trump's logic that although tariffs hurt the US, this is acceptable as long as the tariffs hurt China more.

We can see that the use of economic means such as tariffs for non-economic goals—economic sanctions—has increased massively in recent decades. For example, data from the Global Sanctions Database shows how much economic sanctions in particular have increased over the last ten to 15 years. In doing to, governments are trying to pursue a non-trade policy using trade policy instruments, whether to promote democracy in other countries, to restore human rights, to end a war (for example the sanctions against Russia), to combat terrorism, to resolve a territorial conflict, or to bring about political change. In the past, even military means might have been used for this purpose, and so from this perspective, sanctions represent progress in social history because they do not claim people's lives, at least not in a direct way. But it is always about enforcing a country's own policies against the actual will of other sovereign states—whether they are democratic or not.

Research clearly shows that sanctions can be very powerful means in the sense that they interrupt trade flows and thus cause damage. This is all the more the case the more isolated the sanctioned country is globally. For example, there are studies that show how many children have died due to the West's sanctions against Iraq. This is not a case of a few hundred children, but in some studies shockingly high numbers of up to 200,000. Sanctions are definitely lethal weapons too.

In the past, most sanctions were trade sanctions, but today financial sanctions and travel restrictions have also become important. This too shows how the use of trade policy instruments has increased for reasons of power politics or with the intention of improving the world (for example to enforce human rights).

OUTLOOK: WHY GLOBALIZATION ISN'T OVER

What can we say about the outlook? Formal, institutionalized multilateral systems, in particular the WTO, are suffering an existential crisis. The IMF and the World Bank too are in trouble. If we consider how much money these institutions are currently able to lend, demand for their products has fallen significantly for the time being. The IMF has received a major recapitalization, but potential client countries now have other lenders. They can secure financing from other sources, for example through the new development bank set up by China. We probably have to get used to the fact that the crisis in the system will not disappear in the short and medium term, because the geo-economic tensions in the background—the zero-sum game of power politics—have become more important. Nevertheless, there are megatrends, above all demographics, decarbonization, and digitalization, that further promote globalization because they reduce trading costs and also increase the gains that can be achieved in trade through international movements of capital. This means that because of these megatrends, the need for institutional juridification continues to grow in the background. A second point suggesting that the outlook for an international trading system cannot be too bad is that there are many global commons that can only be regulated globally. Climate change is the most important issue here, but we could also cite the preservation of biodiversity or the fight against terrorism.

Overall, the international trading system should not be seen structurally as in a de-globalization phase, but rather in a transformation phase. This includes the creation of blocs. But there is also something positive behind this creation of blocs, namely the search for models that work. One example would be the idea of a climate club because we have not yet set up global carbon pricing. Whether a climate club is achievable remains another question, but this is at least comparatively more pragmatic and feasible than global carbon pricing. It is also clear that we will see a boom in trade in services as soon as politicians are able to allow more globalization again. Thanks to technological possibilities, many things can now be traded that were previously not tradable. Goods will no longer be the central driver of globalization processes.

Notes

1. See David Ricardo, *On the Principles of Political Economy and Taxation* (London 1817).
2. Jonathan Eaton and Samuel Kortum, "Technology, Geography, and Trade" in *Econometrica*, vol. 70, issue 5 (2001), pp. 1741–1779.
3. Robert Powell, "Absolute and Relative Gains in International Relations Theory" in *The American Political Science Review*, vol. 85, issue 4 (1991), pp. 1303–1320.
4. In the language of game theory, non-cooperation is a dominant strategy.
5. This is an improvement in the international exchange ratio, the so-called "terms of trade (t-o-t)" (the ratio of the export price index to the import price index). If the "t-o-t" increase, real per capita income rises; if they decrease, it falls.
6. This applies as long as the original trading structure remains in place. If the countries swap sectors in which they have

comparative advantages, China's technical progress in its (former) import sector will once again increase prosperity for its trading partners.

7. If individual countries specialize in narrow product niches where they enjoy high market shares, then even small economies can have an influence on world market prices in their export markets. See Gabriel Felbermayr, Benjamin Jung, and Mario Larch, "Optimal tariffs, retaliation, and the welfare loss from tariff wars in the Melitz model" in *Journal of International Economics*, vol. 89 (2013), pp. 13–25.

8. Ralph Ossa und Chang-Tai Hsieh, "A Global View of Productivity Growth in China" in *Journal of International Economics*, vol. 102 (2016), pp. 209–24.

9. The literature speaks of optimal tariffs here. In order for prosperity to really increase, the level of these tariffs must not be too high. Otherwise, the effect of improved exchange conditions will be overcompensated by an excessive reduction in trading volume.

10. Adam Smith, *An Inquiry into the Nature and Causes of the Wealth of Nations* (London, 1776).

11. The concept of "hyperglobalization" was coined by Dani Rodrik. See Dani Rodrik, *The Globalization Paradox: Democracy and the Future of the World Economy* (Oxford: Oxford University Press, 2011).

12. This concept can be traced back to the British weekly magazine *The Economist*. See "Slowbalization: The Future of Global Commerce" in *The Economist*, January 24, 2019.

13. Source: World Bank; author's calculations and graph.

14. Kyle Handley and Nuno Limão, "Trade Policy Uncertainty" in *Annual Review of Economics*, vol. 14, issue 1 (2022), pp. 363–95.

15. Source: Global Trade Alert, University of St. Gallen. Number of new trade policy measures per year (left-hand

graph); share of the number of measures since 2009 (right-hand graph).

16. Fig. 4: * KOF Globalization Index "Economic Openness" **Share of global GDP in % in current US dollars. Source: World Bank; author's calculations and graph.

17. Jeffry Frieden, "The Political Economy of the Globalization Backlash: Sources and Implications" in Luis A.V. Catão and Maurice Obstfeld (eds.), *Meeting Globalization's Challenges* (Princeton: Princeton University Press, 2019).

18. For example Dani Rodrik (see note 11).

CHAPTER 15

CRISIS AS THE ANTIDOTE TO BOREDOM

HANS ULRICH OBRIST AND ADRIAN GHENIE IN CONVERSATION

An edited transcript of the Convoco Art Conversation between Hans Ulrich Obrist and Adrian Ghenie at the Convoco Forum on July 29, 2023, in Salzburg

Hans Ulrich Obrist: All roads of the conversations at this year's Forum lead to Adrian Ghenie. We've been discussing systems in a state of crisis and emergency, and with Adrian we have an artist who has direct experience of a system's collapse, namely the collapse of the communist regime in Romania under Nicolae

Ceaușescu in 1989. Adrian, you were born in 1977 in Baia Mare in Romania. Ceaușescu was in power. His reign began in 1965 with a brief period of liberalization, but by the time you were born, totalitarianism had returned. Your childhood was also marked by years of national austerity, starting in 1981 and leading all the way up to 1989. Can you tell us more about your childhood in Romania?

Adrian Ghenie: Over the last 30 years, I have been reading a lot to understand what happened with the world I was born in. I noticed that in all the explanations of what led to the collapse of the communist world in 1989, one aspect is never addressed: it was boring. The communist regime is essentially a boring environment. It's not the kind of boredom a person feels when not knowing what to do with their afternoon. It's a boredom that goes almost to a molecular level. I remember the Romania of the 1980s, my childhood, as a silence. Everyone, young and old, had this vague idea that everything was somehow decided. The Soviet Union famously found itself in the "Era of Stagnation" under Brezhnev. The Soviets didn't want to use the word "boredom" because it is too subjective, but this boredom, I think, was one of the invisible causes that brought down the communist regime.

As an artist, I too get bored sometimes. Boredom is a battle you have to fight as an individual every day. But communism had this problem as a system, the problem was everywhere, and in my opinion, the system collapsed because of that.

HUO: There is a fascinating book about this collapse by Alexei Yurchak called *Everything Was Forever, Until It Was No More*, which was once recommended to me by the artist and musician Brian Eno. The book is about Soviet socialism being based on paradoxes that were only revealed to the people by the peculiar experience of its collapse:

> To the people who lived in that system the collapse seemed both completely unexpected and completely unsurprising. At the moment of collapse it suddenly became obvious that Soviet life had always seemed simultaneously eternal and stagnating, vigorous and ailing, bleak and full of promise. Although these characteristics may appear mutually exclusive, in fact they were mutually constitutive.[1]

When we spoke yesterday over coffee, I told you about this book by Alexei Yurchak. You then mentioned Svetlana Alexievich, the Nobel Prize-winning writer, and her book, *Second-hand Time*, which was very important to you.

AG: I had a revelation reading that book, because it was the first time I felt that someone actually had a response to why this world collapsed—without necessarily having a real answer. Svetlana Alexievich interviewed hundreds if not thousands of people in the Soviet Union, from ordinary people to academics to military personnel, to show how different the fall of the Soviet Union was for every one of these people. Then I understood that what happened in Eastern Europe during the Soviet time was more complex than we like to believe. It's easy to say, "It was a bad regime, it disappeared, now everybody should be happy." But everyone was not happy. Many people had this nostalgia, including part of my family. It was a strange situation, and somehow it's still lingering. For people like intellectuals who really enjoyed the idea of freedom, the collapse of the communist system was clearly a good thing. But there was a big part of the population for whom that was not clear.

HUO: How did you experience the revolution and the transition to democracy? And what prompted you to paint portraits of Nicolae Ceaușescu?

AG: I was 13 when the revolution happened. It was probably the best TV show I've ever seen. For 72 hours I could follow all the events live, despite living in a small town somewhere in the north. That was very exciting. My first thought as a kid back then was that finally I could eat pineapple. Because of this Ceaușescu guy, I couldn't, but now he was gone, so I could have pineapple. I was really excited that finally this tropical fruit would come into my life. And it wasn't just me—all the kids had a thing about pineapples or bananas. The apples we had were boring in comparison. When pineapples finally arrived about three years later, I queued to get some, but it was all gone before it was my turn. So it happened that I only tried pineapple when I moved to Germany in 2007.

As an adult, and mostly after having left Romania, I felt a need to try and confront myself with "characters" such as Ceaușescu and Stalin. You have to understand that I didn't know, for example, that Stalin was a bad guy until I watched a BBC documentary in 1991. When I was a child we had an encyclopedic dictionary in our house, and my father always told me, "If you don't know something, just look it up in here." Stalin was a great guy in that book. It was a shock to see the BBC documentary and realize that this wasn't the case. I investigated these people by painting their portrait. It is a very strange feeling to actually look at their picture and try to paint them.

HUO: You left Romania and went into a first "exile," but then you came back, and something very important happened: you decided to set up an exhibition space in Cluj called Plan B, an exhibition space that has become legendary and entered art history. Can you tell us more about starting that space?

AG: My whole generation had a phase where we all went to the West, semi-illegal let's say, trying to get a life there. But we failed and returned to Romania completely broke. In that kind of despair, we were asking ourselves "OK, what shall we do now?" This was back in 2000, when Romania was not yet part of the European Union, and everything was really cheap relative to the West. Back then, 100 Deutschmarks was a fortune in Romania. With that money, we could rent an exhibition space for a year, and with another 1,000 Deutschmarks we could run a program for almost two years. A friend of mine who was starting out as a collector said, "I will give you the money." And so, we decided to start a gallery. Today a project like that would be impossible. Cluj is now a city with a completely redeveloped real estate market. You wouldn't find a space to rent for under 3,000 Euros per month. But back then Romania was off-grid and bankrupt enough to allow for this type of artistic experience to happen.

When Romania was admitted to Europe in 2004, there was suddenly a lot of interest in our country. Everybody was curious, and we were ready for it, having created this space. People were so excited to find out about us. They had this very romantic idea, as if they were discovering a band in a garage. We were then invited to the Armory Show in New York City. We installed our small booth, it's the opening, and the four of us are completely anonymous there. But the next morning, I'm taking the subway, and this guy is leaving the *New York Times* behind on his seat. I pick it up, and I see a full-page picture of a work from our booth, with the text "This year, the New York Armory Show has galleries from all over the world, including Transylvania, which, believe it or not, is not a fantasy but a real place with a contemporary art scene." Here I am, having arrived in America only the day before, and there's a work from our artist-run space printed in the *New York Times*. That was a shock.

HUO: Opening this space and having the generosity to put an entire scene on the map reminds me of what happened at Transmission Gallery in Glasgow in the early 1990s with artists such as Christine Borland and Douglas Gordon.

AG: Yes, but desperation is part of it as well. Sometimes you realize that your boat is sinking and that if you're not collaborating with someone else, you will be buried. You have to collaborate for self-preservation.

HUO: And in a way this collaboration led you to find your own language. You eventually decided to stop being part of the gallery, leading to the first phase of your work in which you try to depict the texture of Central Europe. Tell us a bit more about this phase between 2007 and 2009.

AG: Only after I graduated from the Art Academy and left Romania did I realize that my identity is Central European. This is not just a geographic category, it's something very distinct from being Western European or Slavic for example. Central European is a very specific formula for me and hard to describe. If you look at the last 100 years, there is a strange combination going on. At the beginning of the century, Central Europe was one of the most sophisticated parts of the world. From Prague to Vienna to Budapest to Transylvania, one could find the finest of everything. But within 40 years Central Europe became first the stage for the most horrible atrocities and then for the communist regimes. It's almost as if someone had a sadistic plan to take this, culturally speaking, amazingly sophisticated area, and then experiment with it in the worst ways. The most perverted thing is that all of these traumatic events have become a muted element of Central Europe, they became part of the fiber of this place. In Romania, I had a feeling that everyone around me had some sort of compulsive disorder that had its origin in this type of trauma muted over decades. My father, for example, had a big basement, and he couldn't throw anything away. Everything was stored in it until it became a sort of installation. I thought to myself "this is Central European." The basement somehow perfectly described this feeling of layers in the Central European identity. I tried to paint that feeling because I wanted to turn this reality into something artistic that could be felt universally. Like a perfume. Someone living in California, on the opposite side of the world and with very different experiences, should feel and understand that place when viewing my painting.

HUO: A collective memory?

AG: Exactly. That's what I was trying to do. I don't know if it works.

HUO: Of course it works, and it led to your second phase of painting which is less about a specific subject matter and more about painting as a medium. But it's also about clichés that you revisit from an East European perspective.

AG: The communists were always afraid of culture, especially Western culture, because they feared the Romanian people might want to get a taste of the West. And so cultural institutions were only allowed to present parts of Western culture if these were already absolute clichés. For example, there would be endless movies with Charlie Chaplin but no new movies from the 1980s or 1970s. You could watch Buster Keaton as much as you want but nothing contemporary. On the art side, it was all Van Gogh and other eternal and completely safe names. That's why I became obsessed with these clichés and decided to revisit them.

HUO: You call this period your "Darwin phase" because, peculiarly, you ended up looking into Charles Darwin's vomiting syndrome.

AG: Yes, names like Van Gogh and Darwin furnished my childhood and I came to consider them as something uninteresting because they are such a known quantity. In response, I tried to discover details about them that would allow me to find a completely different angle and understanding of these people. In the case of Charles Darwin, I learned in my reading that he had a vomiting syndrome, and so I tried to understand and paint him from that perspective. It's all somehow connected to the idea of texture, which is always difficult to explain because it's based so much on gut feeling. It all came to me when I read in an article that Lenin is going moldy in his mausoleum. From time to time, someone had to remove the blue mold with a little brush. That's when I knew how to paint Lenin.

HUO: You talk often about the role of crisis in painting or art making, and that connects to the Convoco topic. What is crisis for you?

AG: Crisis is the antidote to boredom. Without crisis we are finished. It's the thing we need. I sometimes have the feeling that the West is obsessed with solving crises. Solving a crisis is sometimes a problem in itself. I know this sounds like a paradox, but all the rhetoric about crisis is coming from a managerial perspective, from people who are managing companies and institutions, who are obsessed with solving a crisis. We will always be in a crisis. If I were a politician, I would be careful to automatically present every crisis as a problem. Crises are what keeps us going forward.

HUO: Art history is often a departure point for your work. You said before that during a crisis in painting, you always return to de Kooning and Soutine.

AG: What is a crisis in art? When you get bored. But boredom is a more complex concept than it sounds, because boredom can mean you start to doubt your beliefs or system. Then you have to reactivate yourself. And there are artists like de Kooning or Soutine who always manage to give me this kick—not to exit the crisis but to go even deeper and reach a sort of despair. That is sometimes essential to keep painting. After a certain point, the medium of painting, the act itself, is not interesting. It's exhausting, physical work that I was never fond of. After half an hour I am tired, and to stay for another four I need to enter crisis mode: I have to manufacture a disaster on the canvas by destroying some parts I already liked. I want to bring about a moment of "Oh my God, what did I do?" because I believe that art is not a natural thing to do. We are only doing art because we are in crisis. There is no art without crisis.

HUO: A recurrent theme in your work and your interviews is energy. You say that energy preoccupies you in every painting as it keeps everything together. What is energy?

AG: When I look at a painting I can feel its energy signature in the brushstrokes, probably because I paint myself. If there is a flow to it, then I like the painting. When I feel that the artist took risks, was in crisis, and had to take desperate measures to redo and save the painting, that's what I call energy. The surface of a painting is the diary of the artist's hellish fight. In contrast, it's terrible to look at a painting which is done *alla prima* [on first attempt], where the artist looked at whatever he wanted to paint and then it came out exactly like it. There is no fight there, just virtuosity. But virtuosity is not interesting to me. Virtuosity alone is the definition of boredom.

HUO: Venkatesh Rao recently wrote in a fascinating blog post that there is a kind of "unnarratability" of our times, and that leads me to your third phase, your most recent paintings.[2] Because just as Venkatesh talks about "unnarratability," you have talked about "unpaintability" in the digital era, for example, in the case of the iPhone.

AG: As an artist I am always looking at texture, trying to understand it, and thinking about how to depict texture. A few years ago, I started to paint an iPhone and I realized I was unable to. Why? Because there is no texture, there is only a kind of black hole. I was wondering if I should do an experiment and ask 20 art students to paint an iPhone. I would probably get 20 identical paintings because there is just no texture to this weird thing. I know it sounds funny, you'd think you know its texture—it's shiny, there's plastic, etc.— but you should try to paint it. There is nothing to paint, just black surface. Cezanne made a whole career out of painting apples, but this phone cannot be painted. It drives me crazy that our world is losing its texture. And so the only way to paint an iPhone is to also paint a hand holding the iPhone. A hand has information, depth, and texture.

HUO: We previously had a fascinating conversation about the fact that you feel very strongly about the body language associated with phones. I saw it for myself yesterday when taking the train from Zurich to Salzburg: at least half of the people were on their devices showing a certain body language.

AG: Every historical time has a pose, a body language, or a certain way they wanted to be represented. Today, everywhere you look you see a body inclined towards a phone. It's strangely universal. I don't think there is another defining body language of our time. I call this pose "passive anxiety." It's somehow passive because you're just looking, but at the same time what's coming from there creates anxiety. This "passive anxiety" is defining for me today, and it's how I explain to myself what I see.

HUO: Digital devices also seem to bring about a change of the artist's studio. The studio used to be a place of solitude, but these devices now add a permanent presence of the collective. So there is not only a new body language but also…

AG: …the end of silence. At least in terms of artistic practice, the artist will never be alone again. They will be suspended between this weird desire to be alone and the constant presence of a multitude in their studio. I believe this limbo will change art completely.

If I look at the art made over the last 8,000 years until recently, there is a silence in it. You can see that it was made by people who essentially had silence or solitude. But I think this period is over because our minds will never be like that again. Instead, we will always be connected with something, completely changing the way we do art.

HUO: The last topic I want to address in our conversation today concerns the art system. Artworks and particularly exhibitions are traveling around the world and have an environmental impact, which creates the question whether it would be more sustainable and therefore necessary to find more fixed places for art as we had in the past. You have had this feeling and I think it's a very important intuition. I see many artists right now who say, metaphorically speaking, that they would rather make a garden than an exhibition. It's about long durational projects.

AG: Andy Warhol once said the best art is if you buy land and not destroy it with construction.[3] I agree with that. There is something prophetic in it. I fantasize about an art world that is less international in the sense that we are traveling less. We are in too many places at the same time. I think we should go back to a sort of localism. Our mentality should stay international, but I would like us to work more for the places where we actually live. Many friends of mine live in Cluj, but there are no projects at all. They are constantly flying out to work somewhere else, and then their work is packed up and shipped out again. It's endless traveling. I think it would be much more interesting and sustainable if artists started to develop a mentality that a work has to stay in the places where they live or that they have to relate themselves to the places where they live.

HUO: You have done two paintings for the Chiesa della Madonna della Mazza church in Palermo which will stay fixed there. Can you tell us about the creation of these works?

AG: I met the writer Alessandra Borghese by chance in Paris, and she asked me whether I would be interested in painting for a church. I said, "Yeah, why not." It's a completely different angle, because the work won't move into an exhibition and then a collection. Instead, it must stay in one place. It's a real change, and especially so because churchgoers are an audience outside of the art world and without the elitist element. The whole experience and process of producing that work was incredible. When we had just put the paintings up and fixed them in place, I was sitting in the front doorway of the church smoking a cigarette. We left the door open a bit because it was summer and really hot. The church was not even inaugurated yet, but these two old ladies just came in and started praying in front of one of the paintings. They probably didn't even realize that this was a new painting. Of course, some people will recognize the subject, but there will always be a mystical side which is absent from the art world.

HUO: In all my conversations with artists I always ask about unrealized projects because we know a great deal about architects' unrealized projects—they publish them—but we know very little about those of everyone else. You told me that you dream of a place with frescoes, and I think that connects deeply to the idea of a more sustainable way of working.

AG: Yes, I have very big walls at my place which I would like to decorate with frescoes. I associate frescoes with the idea that something cannot be moved. It's less subject to the caprices of the market or the ego of a collector. It's meant to stay in one place. I think frescoes might have a revival in the future because of this connection with the concept of the local. I never did a fresco, and I have no idea how to do fresco, so I guess I will have to learn how.

HUO: Finally, poetry should be the conclusion of our conversation because reading literature is very important to you. You have a wonderful story about the Romanian visionary Lucian Blaga, who once wrote:

> In dreams, through longings, we can see—
> All latent in the dust of gold
> These forests that perhaps could be—
> But that will never, ever, grow.[4]

Lucian Blaga was nominated for the Nobel Prize for Literature, but for political reasons the Romanian government made it impossible for him to win. Would you tell us your story about Lucian Blaga?

AG: A friend of mine bought an old house in Cluj. And he said to me: "It's full of furniture, do you want to have a look around? Whatever you find you can take for free." So I went, and I found a desk with a secret drawer. In it I discovered a letter from Lucian Blaga to the Central Committee of the Communist Party trying to explain to them why he shouldn't be arrested. I don't know if he ever sent the letter—you can see he was working on it, cutting phrases—but it was kind of moving. Here is a poet who knows that he will be arrested. But he also knows the arrest would create a bit of fuss, and so he thinks he has a small chance of avoiding arrest if he writes the right kind of letter. It's interesting to see him trying to find suitable words, because these were the 1950s and the Communist Party were Stalinist fools. The poet realizes that he cannot write poetry to this absolute idiot, and yet as a poet he cannot do otherwise. And that makes this letter such an interesting piece of literature.

HUO: That's a wonderful conclusion. Thank you, Adrian.

Notes

1 Alexei Yurchak, *Everything Was Forever, Until It Was No More* (Princeton: Princeton University Press, 2005).

2 Venkatesh Rao, *Unnarratability*, https://studio.ribbonfarm.com/p/unnarratability (accessed September 27, 2023).

3 See Andy Warhol, *The Philosophy of Andy Warhol: From A to B and Back Again* (San Diego: Harcourt Brace Jovanovich, 1975), p. 71: "I think having land and not ruining it is the most beautiful art that anybody could ever want to own."

4 Lucian Blaga (1895–1961), "May Gives Itself with Sweet Abandon".

CONTRIBUTORS

Prof. Dr. Marietta Auer has been Director of the Max Planck Institute for Legal History and Legal Theory in Frankfurt am Main since 2020 and is Professor of Private Law and the International and Interdisciplinary Foundations of Law at the Justus Liebig University in Giessen. Since 2021 she has also held an Honorary Professorship at the Goethe University in Frankfurt am Main. Before moving to Frankfurt, after studying law and philosophy in Munich and Harvard and completing her doctorate and postdoctoral qualification in Munich, she held the Chair of Civil Law and Philosophy of Law at the Justus Liebig University in Giessen. From 2016 to 2019 she was Dean of the Law Faculty at the University of Giessen. She turned down offers to move to the University of Bonn and the Bucerius Law School. In 2022 her research was awarded the Gottfried Wilhelm Leibniz Prize of the

German Research Foundation (DFG). Marietta Auer is a member of the National Academy of Sciences Leopoldina and the Academia Europaea. She has also been Vice-President of the German Research Foundation since 2022.

Prof. Dr. Tim Crane is a Professor of Philosophy at Central European University (CEU), Vienna. Before coming to CEU he was Knightbridge Professor of Philosophy at the University of Cambridge and a Fellow of Peterhouse from 2009. Before that he taught at UCL for 19 years and founded the Institute of Philosophy at the University of London as its first Director in 2005. He was educated at the Universities of Durham, York, and Cambridge, where he obtained his Ph.D. in 1989. Crane is the author of many articles on philosophy of mind and metaphysics, and of the following books: *The Mechanical Mind* (1995, 3rd edition 2016), *Elements of Mind* (2001), *The Objects of Thought* (2013), *Aspects of Psychologism* (2014), and *The Meaning of Belief: Religion from an Atheist's Point of View* (2017). He was the editor of the *Routledge Encyclopedia of Philosophy*, and the philosophy consultant editor for the TLS. His work has been translated into Arabic, Chinese, Croatian, French, German, Hungarian, Italian, Japanese, Korean, Persian, Polish, Portuguese,

Romanian, Spanish, and Swedish. Crane is the Director of Research of the Cluster of Excellence, Knowledge in Crisis, a research project funded by the Austrian Science Fund (FWF). He is currently working on the nature of the unconscious and on the nature of belief.

Prof. Gabriel Felbermayr, Ph.D. is Director of the Austrian Institute of Economic Research (WIFO) and a Professor at the Vienna University of Economics and Business. After studying economics and trade at the University of Linz, he went to Florence to pursue his doctoral studies. From 2004 to 2005, he was an Associate Consultant with McKinsey & Co. in Vienna. From 2005 to 2008, he was Assistant Professor at the University of Tübingen. From 2009 to 2010, he held a Chair in International Economics at the University of Hohenheim (Stuttgart). From 2010 to 2019, he led the ifo Center for International Economics at the University of Munich, where he also served as Professor of International Economics. From 2019 to September 2021, he was President of Kiel Institute for the World Economy. At the same time, he held a Chair in Economics and Economic Policy at Kiel University (CAU). Gabriel Felbermayr is a member of the Scientific Advisory Board of the Germany Federal Ministry for Economic Affairs and Climate Action, and the Chairman of the Statistics Council at Statistics Austria. He is Associate Editor at the *European Economic Review*. Gabriel Felbermayr's research focuses on issues of international trade theory and policy, labor market research, European economic integration, and current economic policy issues. He has published a large number of papers in international scholarly journals, policy briefs, and newspapers. His research has been recognized with various awards.

Dr. Corinne Michaela Flick studied both law and literature, taking American studies as her subsidiary, at Ludwig Maximilian University, Munich. She gained her Dr. Phil. in 1989. She has worked as in-house lawyer for Bertelsmann Buch AG and Amazon.com. In 1998 she became General Partner in Vivil GmbH und Co. KG, Offenburg. She is Founder and Chair of the Convoco Foundation. As Editor of Convoco! Editions she has published among others: *Equality in an Unequal World* (2023), *How much Freedom must we Forgo to be Free?* (2022), *New Global Alliances: Institutions, Alignments and Legitimacy in the Contemporary World* (2021), *The Standing of Europe in the New Imperial World Order* (2020), *The Multiple Futures of Capitalism* (Convoco! Editions, 2019), *The Common Good in the 21st Century* (2018), *Authority in Transformation* (2017), *Power and* its *Paradoxes* (2016), *To Do or Not To Do—Inaction as a Form of Action* (2015), *Dealing with Downturns: Strategies in Uncertain Times* (2014). She was awarded the 2023 Prize for Understanding and Tolerance by the Jewish Museum Berlin. Since October 2023, she has been Honorary Visiting Professor and Professorial Fellow of the Humanities Research Institute at the University of Buckingham.

Prof. Dr. Dr. h.c. Clemens Fuest (b. 1968) is President of the ifo Institute–Leibniz Institute for Economic Research at the University of Munich e.V., Executive Director of CESifo GmbH, Professor of Economics and Public Finance at Ludwig Maximilian University, Munich, and Director of the Center for Economic Studies (CES) at LMU. He is among other posts a member of the Advisory Board to the German Federal Ministry of Finance, the European Academy of Sciences and Arts, the Scientific Advisory Board of the Market Economy Foundation (Kronberger Kreis) and the Foundation for Family Businesses in Germany and Europe.

Previously, he was President of the IIPF (International Institute of Public Finance e.V.) from 2018 to 2021 and member of the Franco-German Board of Economic Experts from 2019 to 2022. In 2013 he received the Gustav Stolper Award of the Verein für Socialpolitik (Social Policies Society, VfS), in 2019 he received the 2018 Hanns Martin Schleyer Award, and in 2023 he was awarded the Bavarian Maximilian Order for Science and Art. In 2017 Clemens Fuest received an honorary doctorate from the Karlsruhe Institute of Technology (KIT).

His research areas are economic and financial policy, international taxation, tax policy, and European integration. Before his appointment at Munich, he was a professor at the Universities of Cologne (2001–08), Oxford (2008–13), and Mannheim (2013–16). He is the author of a number of books and has published many commentaries and byline articles on contemporary questions of economic policy in national and international journals. He also writes for newspapers such as *Handelsblatt, Frankfurter Allgemeine Zeitung, Die Zeit, Süddeutsche Zeitung, WirtschaftsWoche, Financial Times,* and *The Wall Street Journal.*

Adrian Ghenie was born in 1977 in Baia Mare, Romania. Ghenie studied at the University of Art and Design in Cluj Napoca, and in 2005 he co-founded Galeria Plan B, a production and exhibition space for contemporary art. Since 2013 Ghenie has lived and worked in Berlin.

He was selected to represent Romania at the 56th Venice Biennale in 2015. His recent solo exhibitions include shows at Pace Gallery, New York; Galerie Judin, Berlin; Tim Van Laere Gallery, Antwerp; the State Hermitage Museum, Saint Petersburg; and Palazzo Cini, Venice.

In 2022 two site-specific paintings by the artist were permanently installed in the historic setting of Chiesa della Madonna della Mazza, Palermo, in an independent project curated by Alessandra Borghese. Alongside his paintings, the artist has created several installations: *The Dada Room* (2010), now in the permanent collection of S.M.A.K., Ghent, and *The Darwin Room* (2013–14), in the collection of the Centre Pompidou. His work is held in important public collections including those of the Centre Pompidou, Paris; Tate Modern, London; San Francisco Museum of Modern Art; Metropolitan Museum of Modern Art, New York; and The Long Museum, Shanghai.

Prof. Dr. Dr. h.c. Birke Häcker has been Schlegel Chair in Civil Law, Common Law, and Comparative Law, and Director of the Institute of International and Comparative Private Law at the University of Bonn since 2023. Prior to taking up her position, she was, inter alia, a Fellow of All Souls College, Oxford from

2001 to 2008 and from 2011 to 2016; from 2011 to 2016 a Senior Research Fellow at the Max Planck Institute for Tax Law and Public Finance in Munich; in 2016 she took up the Statutory Chair in Comparative Law at the University of Oxford and Professorial Fellow at Brasenose College; and from 2018 to 2022 she was Director of Oxford's Institute of European and Comparative Law. As an undergraduate, she obtained a dual legal education, reading jurisprudence at Oxford as well as German law at the Universities of Tübingen and Bonn. Her Oxford D.Phil. was in comparative private law. She publishes on a broad range of topics in English and German private law, comparative law, and legal history

Prof. Dr. Peter M. Huber gained his Ph.D. Dr. jur. in 1987 and his postdoctoral qualification in constitutional and administrative law in 1991. He was Professor of Public Law in Augsburg. In 1992–2001 he was Professor of Constitutional and Administrative Law, European Law, Public, Commercial, and Environmental Law in Jena. He was Chair of Public Law and European Integration Law in Bayreuth from 2001 to 2002. Since 2002 he has held the Chair of Public Law and Political Philosophy in Munich. Among his publications are: *Grundrechtsschutz durch*

Organisation und Verfahren als Kompetenzproblem in der Gewaltenteilung und im Bundesstaat (1987); *Konkurrenzschutz im Verwaltungsrecht* (1991); *Recht der Europäischen Integration* (second edition, 2002); *Klarere Verantwortungsteilung von Bund, Ländern und Kommunen?* (2004); *Staat und Wissenschaft* (2008); *Beiträge zu Juristenausbildung und Hochschulrecht* (2010). He is Joint Editor of *The Max Planck Handbook in European Public Law,* vols. I–IV (Oxford University Press, 2017–2023) and *GG*, vols. I–III (Commentary on the German Basic Law, with Andreas Voßkuhle, 8th edition, 2024). From 2009 to 2010 Professor Huber was Interior Minister for Thuringia, and from 2010–2023 Judge in Germany's Federal Constitutional Court.

Prof. Dr. Stefan Korioth gained his doctorate in law in 1990 and completed his postdoctoral qualification in public and constitutional law. From 1996 to 2000 he was Professor of Public Law, Constitutional History, and Theory of Government at the University of Greifswald. In 2000 he accepted the Chair of Public and Ecclesiastical Law at Ludwig Maximilian University, Munich. His publications include *Integration und Bundesstaat* (1990), *Der Finanzausgleich zwischen Bund und Ländern* (1997), *Grundzüge des*

Staatskirchenrechts (with B. Jean d'Heur, 2000), *Das Bundesverfassungsgericht* (with Klaus Schlaich, 12th edition, 2021), *Staatsrecht I* (6th edition, 2022), and *Deutsche Verfassungsgeschichte* (2023).

Prof. Dr. Martin Korte, born in 1964, is director of the Zoological Institute and Head of the Cellular Neurobiology department at the TU Braunschweig. He also heads the Neuroinflammation and Neurodegeneration Working Group at the Helmholtz Center for Infection Research in Braunschweig. Among other things, he is a member of the Berlin-Brandenburg Academy of Sciences (BBAW) where he is also an elected board member. He was a founding member of Die Junge Akademie at the Leopoldina and the BBAW. He received the Ars Legendi Faculty Prize for innovative teaching in 2014 and the North German Science Prize (2nd place) in 2022. His research areas are the neural basis of learning and forgetting. Before his appointment to Braunschweig, he was a working group leader at the Max Planck Institute of Neurobiology in Martinsried near Munich and completed his postdoctoral qualification at the LMU Munich. He is the author of several books. His latest book, *Frisch im Kopf,* was published by DVA in 2023.

Prof. Dr. Jörn Leonhard is Chair of Western European History at the Albert Ludwig University of Freiburg, and an author. Having studied history, political science, and German philology in Heidelberg and Oxford, he received his Ph.D. in 1998 and completed his postdoctoral qualification at Heidelberg University in 2004. From 1998 to 2003 he was a Fellow and Tutor at Oxford University; Visiting Research Fellow at the Alexander von Humboldt Foundation in the German-American Center for Visiting Scholars in Washington, D.C. in 2001; Fellow of the Royal Historical Society London since 2002; and Senior Research Fellow at the Institute for Contemporary History of the Historisches Kolleg in Munich from 2016 to 2017. From 2007 to 2012 he was Director of the School of History at the Freiburg Institute for Advanced Studies (FRIAS) and in 2012/13 Visiting Professor at Harvard University. His research and publications have received multiple awards, among them the Leibniz Prize in 2024. His most recent English publication is *Pandora's Box: A History of the First World War* (2018). Jörn Leonhard has been full member of the Heidelberg Academy of Sciences and Humanities since 2015 and Honorary Fellow of Wadham College, Oxford University, since 2019.

Prof. Dr. Timo Meynhardt holds the Dr. Arend Oetker Chair of Business Psychology and Leadership at the HHL Leipzig Graduate School of Management. He is Managing Director of the Center for Leadership and Values in Society at the University of St. Gallen, where he obtained his doctorate and postdoctoral qualification in business administration. For several years, he was Practice Expert at McKinsey & Company. Timo Meynhardt's work focuses on public value management and leadership, combining psychology and business management in his research and teaching. He is co-developer of the Leipzig leadership model and co-publisher of the *Public Value Atlas* for Switzerland and Germany, which aims at making transparent the social benefits of companies and organizations (www.gemeinwohlatlas.de; www.gemeinwohl.ch). His Public Value Scorecard provides a management tool to measure and analyze the creation of public value. He is also Co-founder and Jury Member of the Public Value Awards for Startups.

Hans Ulrich Obrist (b. 1968, Zurich, Switzerland) is Artistic Director of the Serpentine in London and Senior Advisor at LUMA Arles. Prior to this, he was the Curator of the Musée d'Art Moderne de la Ville de Paris. Since his first show "World Soup (The Kitchen

Show)" in 1991, he has curated more than 350 exhibitions. His recent shows include "Enzo Mari" at Triennale Milano (2020) and "WORLDBUILDING" at Centre Pompidou Metz (2023) and Julia Stoschek Collection Düsseldorf (2022). In 2011 Obrist received the CCS Bard Award for Curatorial Excellence, and in 2015 he was awarded the International Folkwang Prize, and most recently he was honored by the Appraisers Association of America with the 2018 Award for Excellence in the Arts. Obrist's recent publications include *Ways of Curating* (2015), *The Age of Earthquakes* (2015), *Lives of the Artists, Lives of Architects* (2015), *The Extreme Self: Age of You* (2021), *140 Ideas for Planet Earth* (2021), *Edouard Glissant: Archipelago* (2021), *James Lovelock: Ever Gaia* (2023) *Remember to Dream* (2023), and *Une vie in Progress* (2023).

Prof. Dr. Dr. h.c. Monika Schnitzer is Professor of Comparative Economics at the Ludwig Maximilian University of Munich (LMU). Since October 2022, she has been Chairwoman of the German Council of Economic Experts, of which she has been a council member since April 2020. In January 2023, she became Co-Chair of the Franco-German Council of Economic Experts. She received her doctorate and postdoctoral qualification from the University of

Bonn and conducted research at Boston University, MIT, Stanford University, Yale University, University of California, Berkeley, and Harvard University. From 2006 to 2009 she was Dean of the Economics Faculty at LMU. Her research focuses on innovation, competition, and multinational companies. Her work has been published in the *American Economic Review*, the *American Economic Journal: Economic Policy*, and the *Journal of the European Economic Association*, among others.

Monika Schnitzer has been active in policy consulting for more than 20 years, including as a member of the Scientific Advisory Board of the Federal Ministry for Economic Affairs and Climate Protection and as a member of the Economic Advisory Group on Competition Policy at the Directorate General for Competition of the European Commission. From 2011 to 2019 she was Deputy Chair of the Expert Commission for Research and Innovation. Monika Schnitzer was elected a member of the Bavarian Academy of Sciences in 2008, a member of the Academia Europaea in 2016 and a member of the Leopoldina, Germany's National Academy of Sciences, in 2023. She has been a Fellow of the European Economic Association since 2008. From 2013 to 2014 she was designated Chair of the Verein für Socialpolitik, and from 2015 to 2016 she was its

Chair. In 2005 she was awarded the Federal Order of Merit on Ribbon and in 2012 she was awarded the Bavarian Order of Merit. In 2022 she received the Gustav Stolper Prize of the Verein für Socialpolitik and the European Medal of the Free State of Bavaria. The University of Kiel awarded her an honorary doctorate in 2022.

Prof. Dr. Dr. h.c. Wolfgang Schön studied law and economics at the University of Bonn. He was Professor at the University of Bielefeld from 1992 to 1996, and from 1996 to 2002 at the University of Bonn. Since 2002 he has been Director and Scientific Member of the Max Planck Institute for Tax Law and Public Finance in Munich. He is Honorary Professor at Ludwig Maximilian University Munich; member of the Global Law Faculty, New York University; and International Research Fellow, University of Oxford Centre of Business Taxation. From 2008 to 2014 Prof. Schön was Vice-President of the Max Planck Society. Since 2014 he has been Vice-President of the German Research Foundation (DFG). He has published numerous works on German and European company law, competition law, and tax law.

Prof. Dr. Moritz Schularick is President of the Kiel Institute for the World Economy and Professor of Economics at Sciences Po, Paris. He is an elected member of the Academy of Sciences of Berlin and a Research Professor at New York University. In 2015/16 he held the Alfred Grosser Chair at Sciences Po. Previously, he taught at the Free University of Berlin, and was a Visiting Professor at the University of Cambridge. He is one of the recipients of the 2022 Leibniz Prize. In 2018 he received the Gossen Prize of the German Economic Association. He is a Fellow of the Institute for New Economic Thinking and a Managing Editor of Europe's most important policy journal, *Economic Policy*, a joint initiative between Sciences Po, CEPR, and CESIfo. He is a frequent consultant to central banks and contributes to public debates across different media. His research spans macroeconomics, finance, international economics, and economic history and has been published in *American Economic Review, Quarterly Journal of Economics, Review of Economic Studies, Journal of Political Economy, Journal of Monetary Economics, Journal of International Economics*, and several other journals. His research is supported by major grants from the European Research Council, the German Research Foundation (DFG), and the Institute for New Economic Thinking.

Prof. Dr. Claudia Wiesner is Professor of Political Science at Fulda University of Applied Sciences, a member of the Board of Directors at the Point Alpha Research Institute, and Adjunct Professor in Political Science at Jyväskylä University (Finland). She has been a Visiting Fellow at institutions such as the Minda de Gunzburg Centre for European Studies at Harvard University, New York University, the Robert Schumann Centre for Advanced Studies at the European University Institute (EUI), and the Berlin Social Sciences Centre (WZB). Wiesner's main research focuses on Europe in the world and the comparative study of democracy and governance in the EU, putting particular emphasis on the related concepts, ideas, and theories. She is the Principal Investigator of the Jean Monnet Network "Debating Europe" and of the international projects "Transnational Governance and Human Rights" and "Practising Transnational Politics." Moreover, she chairs the ECPR Standing Group "Political Concepts." She has published with publishers such as Palgrave Macmillan, Routledge, Springer, and Nomos and journal special issues and articles in journals such as *Contemporary Political Theory, Journal of European Integration, Leviathan, Politics and Governance, Politische Vierteljahresschrift, Redescriptions, Parliaments, Estates and Representation, Zeitschrift für Vergleichende*

Politikwissenschaft, and *Zeitschrift für Politikwissenschaft.* Her most recent books are *Politicisation, Democratisation and Identity Formation in the EU* (Routledge, 2024) and *The War Against Ukraine and the EU: Facing New Realities* (Palgrave Macmillan, 2024, ed. Claudia Wiesner and Michèle Knodt).

EQUALITY IN AN UNEQUAL WORLD *2023*

ISBN: 978-1-9163673-6-4

With contributions by: Marietta Auer, Paul Collier, Gabriel Felbermayr, Francisco H. G. Ferreira, Clemens Fuest, Raji Jayaraman, Francis Kéré, Kai A. Konrad, Stefan Korioth, Jörn Leonhard, Timo Meynhardt, Hans Ulrich Obrist, Christoph G. Paulus, Mathias Risse, Wolfgang Schön, Claudia Wiesner, Jonathan Wolff

HOW MUCH FREEDOM MUST WE FORGO TO BE FREE? *2022*

ISBN: 978-1-9163673-4-0

With contributions by: Bazon Brock, Tim Crane, Gabriel Felbermayr, Clemens Fuest, Birke Häcker, Martha Jungwirth, Bruno Kahl, Stefan Korioth, Jörn Leonhard, Rudolf Mellinghoff, Timo Meynhardt, Hans Ulrich Obrist, Philipp Pattberg, Herbert A. Reitsamer, Monika Schnitzer, Sven Simon, Claudia Wiesner, Peter Wittig, Hildegard Wortmann

NEW GLOBAL ALLIANCES: INSTITUTIONS, ALIGNMENTS AND LEGITIMACY IN THE CONTEMPORARY WORLD *2021*

ISBN: 978-1-9163673-2-6

With contributions by: Maha Hosain Aziz, Bazon Brock, Garrett Wallace Brown, Udo Di Fabio, Clemens Fuest, Eugénia C. Heldt, Stefan Korioth, Jörn Leonhard, Rudolf Mellinghoff, Timo Meynhardt, Stefan Oschmann, Christoph G. Paulus, Gisbert Rühl, Wolfgang Schön, Sven Simon, Lothar H. Wieler

THE STANDING OF EUROPE IN THE NEW IMPERIAL WORLD ORDER *2020*

ISBN: 978-1-9163673-0-2

With contributions by: Fredrik Erixon, Gabriel Felbermayr, Birke Häcker, Matthias Karl, Parag Khanna, Kai A. Konrad, Stefan Korioth, Jörn Leonhard, Timo Meynhardt, Hans Ulrich Obrist with Edi Rama, Stefan Oschmann, Christoph G. Paulus, Rupprecht Podszun, Jörg Rocholl, Sven Simon, Yael Tamir, Roberto Viola, Claudia Wiesner

THE MULTIPLE FUTURES OF CAPITALISM *2019*
ISBN: 978-0-9931953-8-9

THE COMMON GOOD IN THE 21st CENTURY *2018*
ISBN: 978-0-9931953-6-5

AUTHORITY IN TRANSFORMATION *2017*
ISBN: 978-0-9931953-4-1

POWER AND ITS PARADOXES *2016*
ISBN: 978-0-9931953-2-7

TO DO OR NOT TO DO—INACTION AS A FORM OF ACTION *2015*

ISBN: 978-0-9931953-0-3

DEALING WITH DOWNTURNS: STRATEGIES IN UNCERTAIN TIMES *2014*

ISBN: 978-0-9572958-8-9

COLLECTIVE LAW-BREAKING—A THREAT TO LIBERTY *2013*

ISBN: 978-0-9572958-5-8

WHO OWNS THE WORLD'S KNOWLEDGE? *2012*
ISBN: 978-0-9572958-0-3

CAN'T PAY, WON'T PAY? SOVEREIGN DEBT AND THE CHALLENGE OF GROWTH IN EUROPE *2011*
ISBN: 978-0-9572958-3-4